The Goodness Within

The Goodness Within

Reaching Out to Troubled Teens
with Love and Compassion

Mark Redmond

Paulist Press
New York/Mahwah, N.J.

The chapter "Faith and Change" is reprinted with permission from the Sept. 10, 2001 issue of *America,* and the chapter "Loss" is reprinted with permission from the May 6, 2002 issue. Copyright by *America.* The chapter "Forgiveness" is reprinted with permission from the March 12, 1999 issue of *Commonweal,* and the chapter "Remembering What Is Important" is reprinted from the April 19, 2002 issue. Copyright by *Commonweal.*

Names of children and youth, and some of the adult staff with whom I worked, have been changed for both legal reasons and privacy.

Scripture extracts are taken from the New Revised Standard Version, Copyright © 1989, by the Division of Christian Education of the National Council of the Churches of Christ in the United States of America and reprinted by permission of the publisher.

Book design by Lynn Else
Cover design by Trudi Gershenov

Library of Congress Cataloging-in-Publication Data

Redmond, Mark V., 1949–
    The goodness within : reaching out to troubled teens with love and compassion / Mark Redmond
        p.   cm.
    ISBN 0-8091-4186-8 (alk. paper)
    1. Church work with teenagers. 2. Teenagers—Religious life. I. Title.
BV4447 .R398 2004
259'.23—dc22

                                                            2003019310

Published by Paulist Press
997 Macarthur Boulevard
Mahwah, New Jersey 07430

www.paulistpress.com

Printed and bound in the
United States of America

Contents

For Marybeth

Acknowledgments

There are many people to thank who have made this book possible. I was fortunate to have many excellent teachers and mentors during my career working with young people. These include Pauline Ceccarelli, Mike Duggan, Poul Jensen, Bob McMahon, Luis Medina, Mary Odom, Chris Pardo, and Dr. Howard Polsky—thank you for advising me, encouraging me, and taking me under your wing. I learned much from each of you.

I am grateful to the editors at *America, Commonweal, New Works Review,* the *New York Times,* and the *Stamford Advocate* for publishing my work.

Thank you to Father Michael Hunt, Father Lawrence Boadt, and Paul McMahon at Paulist Press for taking a chance on me.

I am indebted to Joe Donnelly, Steve Yarri, and Peter Cunningham for reviewing my manuscript and coming up with many helpful suggestions. I am also deeply thankful to the late Sister Thelma Hall, my spiritual director for many years, who always encouraged me to write.

I am blessed with two wonderful children. Aiden, age seventeen, has a warmth, enthusiasm, generosity, and energy that inspire me daily. I often think that God rewarded me for my decades of work with at-risk teenagers by giving me a son like you. And Liam, as I am writing this, is just shy of his first birthday. I have every hope and expectation that you too will turn out to be as good a person as your older brother.

And I thank God every day for my wife Marybeth. She is a tremendous support for me, everything I could ever ask for in a life companion. She was the driving force behind this book in many ways. She has been a great enthusiast, not only throughout the writing of this book, but in every aspect of my life. My everlasting gratitude and love go to you.

Introduction

I am standing in a large courtyard. It resembles one you would see in an old European city. I notice teenage boys standing at different points along the perimeter of the courtyard. They do not know each other, but they begin to exchange menacing looks, followed by trash talk. "Who are you looking at? What do you want? Do you want to mess with me?" Then they begin to walk toward each other. I have witnessed scenes like this so many times in real life that I know they are about to brawl. And the conflict is over nothing, absolutely nothing— kids fighting for the sake of fighting, and they don't even know why. I am very familiar with this scenario from my work with teenagers.

I feel I have to do something to stop the senseless violence about to begin. So I run over and focus in on one young man, trying to guide him away from the pack. He starts to go with me, but he keeps looking over my shoulder at the others, spewing threats and curses. He has the look of hate and anger on his face. I keep trying to talk him out of fighting, leading him away from the others, but the anger inside of him is intense. It is as if part of him wants to listen to me, but another, stronger part wants to battle.

In desperation I shout, if not scream, "Look in the mirror! Look in the mirror!" I believe if I can get him to see what he is doing, the senselessness of it all, he will stop.

And then I say to him, "You're good. You're a good person."

And when he hears those words, the hatred in his face dissipates. He gradually begins to turn away from the other boys,

*from the fight about to erupt, and instead casts his gaze toward
me.*

"I am a good person," he says. "I am good, right?"
"Yes, you are," I reply. "You are good."
And he no longer feels the need to fight.

I have worked with and counseled troubled young men and
women since 1981. Many of them were like the young man in
that dream—filled with rage, ready to strike out in violence,
easily influenced by peer pressure, unable to listen to sound
advice from responsible adults, and headed straight for trouble.

In truth, *all* young people, even the best of them, have these
tendencies to some degree. The question is how we adults can
get through to young people, how we can help them to walk
away from danger, how we can help them to make good decisions, how we can help them to be strong enough to stand up
to peer pressure, how we can help to heal the anger and fear
and loneliness that exist within them. Our responsibility is to
help them to look in the mirror, so to speak, so they can see not
only their actions but, on a deeper level, their own core of
goodness—the goodness within. I believe that when a young
person, or anyone for that matter, is able to do this, there is no
longer any desire to harm others or to harm oneself. The result
is peace and healing, both inside and out.

This book is about helping adolescents to discover their
own worth, dignity, and goodness. It is for parents and anyone
else concerned about the youth of our world today. The book
is really a collection of stories—true stories about young men
and women I've worked with and known, and about situations
I have faced with them. I believe that through stories we learn
certain core truths that no "how-to" manual can impart.

Jesus told stories to illustrate the most important aspects of
his message. I follow his example in this regard. It is my hope

that through the power of story, parents and others who interact with young people will be empowered to pass on the light of healing, friendship, and love, and help them to experience the goodness within.

Commitment

One of the tenets of the Christian faith is that God does not give up on us. He just does not. We can wander away, make all kinds of mistakes, mess things up, and forget what is important, but the "Hound of Heaven" is relentless. God stays after us. We are never far out of his sight. Not because he wants to "get" us, but because he loves us. He wants us to be happy.

In the same way, it is up to us to remain faithful to the young people God puts in our lives, whether they are our own children, nieces, nephews, our students, or those we minister to in a youth group or parish. We have to especially seek out and stay faithful to those who appear to be on a destructive path. These are the ones we have to stick with, no matter what.

If you are in contact with a young person who is involved in dangerous activities such as use of drugs or alcohol, drug dealing, drinking and driving, inappropriate sexual relations, gang membership, or associating with a negative peer group— the first and most important step in the process of helping him or her is your sense of commitment. The same is true for a young person engaged in self-destructive behaviors such as anorexia, bulimia, or cutting themselves. The adult must take the position, "I'm going to stand by this young person, no matter what it takes, no matter how long it takes."

Adults must take a serious stance toward activities like drug use, sexual activity, eating disorders, and so on. They should not fall prey to rationalizations such as, "She'll grow out of this behavior....It's just adolescence....Boys will be boys....The apple doesn't fall far from the tree, and his father was just like that as a teenager, and he turned out fine." Adults must face up to the fact that it is a completely different and more dangerous world than the one they faced a generation ago. The stakes are much higher for teenagers today, the margins of error are narrower. Guns are much more prevalent. There is AIDS. The prospects of succeeding economically without a high school diploma, much less a college degree, are slim. I've attended too many funerals of adolescents during the last twenty-two years to have any illusion that "growing out of it" is any real solution. I know too many teenagers, now adults, who presently live in prisons, drug rehabs, and homeless shelters. The long-term consequences for negative behavior are real, often severe, and sometimes lethal.

The adult has to make the commitment in mind and heart to the young person. Everything else flows from that.

"Yo man, I popped him, I popped that sucker."

That was my introduction to Tony. He was explaining to me how he had just struck the owner of the Harlem hardware store in which he was employed, or more correctly as of that moment, formerly employed. Tony was staying at Covenant House, the Times Square shelter for homeless and runaway teenagers where I had just started working as a full-time volunteer. The year was 1981.

Being new to this line of work, I had no idea if Tony was typical of the young people living at Covenant House, but in time I found out that he was: eighteen years old, African American, born and raised in a poor and dangerous New York City neighborhood, and from a broken home that relied on welfare to survive. I volunteered full-time at Covenant House for the next two years, and I heard some variation of that history hundreds of times. Some of these kids were tossed out of their house because their parents were fed up with their behavior, but the more likely scenario was one in which the family gradually dissolved—parent(s) in jail, in a drug rehab, addicted and on the streets, in a psychiatric hospital, and so on. This left the kids to fend for themselves, and they often spent months or even years living an itinerant existence, staying with various friends and relatives. But those situations are always temporary; friends and relatives usually get tired of taking care of a teenager who isn't theirs, particularly a teenager who probably isn't used to structure and adult supervision. Covenant House was the place of last resort, somewhere to go when there were no more friends or relatives left to take you in.

All Tony told us when he arrived at Covenant House was that his mother was in North Carolina, his father had a job somewhere in the city, he wasn't in touch with either of them, and that he had spent several years in the city's foster care system. Our plan for Tony was to help him find another job and then help him find an apartment so he would be able to live independently.

The Covenant House administration expected this to be accomplished within sixty days for each youth, ninety at the max. It was an almost impossible task, but those of us on the front lines tried anyway. In fact, I did help Tony find another job. But he lost that one too. Then he showed up one night at Covenant House blasted out of his mind. He placed a bag of angel dust—the street drug of choice at that time—on a counselor's desk and left. That was the last time he stepped foot in Covenant House, and for all I knew, it would be my last encounter with him. It wasn't.

One morning about a year later I was walking through Times Square, heading for work at Covenant House. The Times Square of that era was not the Times Square we know today.

There was no Disney. No All-Star Café. No state-of-the-art multiplex cinema. It was seedy, really seedy. It was the core of the pornography industry, certainly for New York City, if not for the country. Dozens of strip joints and peep shows lined 42nd Street and the adjoining blocks. Prostitutes worked the street brazenly, without any fear of arrest. Drugs were sold openly. Small storefront shops sold weapons.

"Girls, girls, girls…totally nude…come inside and see."

I recognized his voice as soon as I heard it: Tony. He stood in front of a strip club, pressing fliers into the hands of passing pedestrians. Before I even had time to avoid him, he was pressing a flier into my hands, and our eyes locked.

For a brief moment there was nothing but surprise on Tony's face, and I probably registered the same. I felt extremely awkward, embarrassed for him. He quickly pulled the flier back, trying to hide the stack of them behind his back. He obviously hoped I had somehow not noticed what he was now doing for a job. He then flashed an awkward smile.

"Mark Redmond. How are you?"

"I'm good, Tony. How are you?"

"Great, I'm just great," he responded. "Are you still working at Covenant House?"

"Yes I am. I've been there almost a year now."

"That's great. How is Dudley? And Patty?" They were counselors he knew.

"They're good," I replied. "I'll tell them you were asking for them."

"Yeah, tell them I said hi."

I told Tony I would, and then there was another awkward moment as we each fished for a quick way out of this chance meeting. I broke the silence when I told him I really had to be at work within the next few minutes. We shook hands. As I crossed 8th Avenue I could hear him behind me, *"Come on in and see the lovely ladies...totally naked...come on in."*

For all I knew, that would be my last encounter with Tony. It wasn't.

Four years later I was at a fundraising event for Part of the Solution, a South Bronx soup kitchen for homeless adults. The event was held at a convent in Greenwich Village. People milled about chatting and sipping wine. I had left Covenant House three years earlier, had married recently and was running a program for street kids in Brooklyn. A lot of my old Covenant House friends and coworkers were at the party. About halfway through the night I heard the booming voice of Fr. Jim Joyce, a Jesuit prison chaplain at Rikers Island.

"Anyone here know Tony T_____?"

I happened to be chatting at that moment with Gerry Stuhlman, who had also volunteered with me at Covenant House. When we heard Fr. Jim we halted our conversation, for we both knew Tony; Gerry had also been his counselor. We both yelled across the room to Fr. Jim, "We know him." Fr. Jim worked his way across the crowded room, which wasn't hard to do since he was about 300 pounds and 6'4".

"He's in jail," said Fr. Jim. "I've had a couple of conversations with him, and he told me no one has visited him. Nobody from his family. None of his friends. And he mentioned that he used to live at Covenant House."

I looked at Gerry. "Why don't we go see him some Saturday?"

Gerry agreed.

Two weeks later Gerry and I traveled to Rikers Island prison, which is in the Queens borough of New York City. Neither of us had ever been there. I've been there many times since then, and it is an unbelievable hassle to get in to see a prisoner. It takes at least two hours of buses, searches, and waiting in order to see a prisoner for one hour. And it takes two more hours afterward to get out of there. Fr. Jim always insisted that the people in charge of Rikers do that on purpose, to discourage visitors. Whatever the case, Gerry and I finally made it into the cavernous room that is the Rikers Island visiting center. We sat side by side at a small table, waiting for Tony. Scores of other prisoners, all dressed in drab green uniforms, sat at other tables. Male prisoners held hands with female visitors. Young children were there to see their fathers. Parents sat across from their imprisoned sons. Prison is always sad, depressing. I guess that's why Jesus held charity toward prisoners in such high esteem. ("For I was hungry and you gave me food, I was thirsty and you gave me something to drink…I was sick and you took care of me, I was in prison and you visited me" [Matt 25:35–36].)

Eventually I spotted Tony being escorted into the visiting area by a guard. Gerry and I had not given him any prior notice whatsoever, and I later learned that a prisoner is simply told by guards that he has a visitor, without any other specifics, such as a name. So Tony wandered through the aisles, the look on his face suggesting, "Who the heck is here to see me?" I could see him scanning the room for a familiar face, and when he saw ours, his face lit up. He showed the wide grin I remembered so well from years before. He was ecstatic and shocked. He hugged each of us, saying over and over again, "I can't believe this! I can't believe you guys!"

We joked around for the first few minutes, laughing, and Tony asked us about certain counselors from Covenant House and how they were doing. We updated him on all the gossip and we reminisced about our experiences there, ours from the perspective of staff, his as a youth living there. I then asked him about the conditions in jail. He told us about the lousy food, what his daily routine was like, tales of guards on the take, fights he'd won and lost, and his time in "the hole" (solitary confinement).

Eventually one of us asked Tony what he was arrested for, and he told us for dealing drugs. I asked him how many of the prisoners in Rikers were there because of drugs. He smiled wryly and answered, "We're all here because of drugs," but promised us he was determined never to do or sell drugs again.

Tony predicted he'd be sent upstate soon, where he'd spend the next one and a half to four and a half years. I asked that he send me his address when he arrived there, and I gave him mine. Before we knew it, a guard was over at our table telling us that we had five minutes left in our hour. Gerry and I hugged him goodbye. We left through one door, he through another.

Tony surprised me by writing when he made it upstate. I wrote back and we corresponded for the next several years. His letters were always about some incident that landed him in the hole, usually a fight he'd had with another inmate. Every letter included a statement of his determination to turn a new leaf once he was released, to stay away from drugs and street life and to never go to jail again. Every letter also included the following request: "Please send me some Little Debbie's® cupcakes." Which is exactly what I did; with each letter to Tony I would enclose a package of Little Debbie's, for which he would later write me that he was eternally grateful.

Through these letters I also learned much about Tony's early life and family. It turned out he was the youngest of five children, born in North Dakota when his father was in the Air Force. The family moved to the South Bronx, where his dad was originally from, when Tony was three. His father found a job at the Post Office and then became a Court Clerk. But his parents divorced when Tony was seven, and then things started falling apart. His mother was awarded custody of all five children, and she went on public assistance. She moved her family from the Bronx to Brooklyn, then back to the Bronx, and then finally to the projects in Harlem. Then Tony's mother decided to move to North Carolina to follow a preacher, leaving the children behind. Tony's father moved into the projects to be with his five children. Tony was age ten, and he said his behavior, which had never been very good, deteriorated rapidly. He frequently refused to go to school, and when he was in school he was often suspended for assaulting teachers and peers. He was removed from home and placed in the foster care system, in a group home in upstate New York. He stayed for two and a half years. He did very poorly there and was transferred to a group home in midtown Manhattan. He was now age thirteen and using beer and pot on a regular basis. He lived in the group home until his eighteenth birthday. At that time group homes were legally allowed to discharge youngsters when they reached age eighteen, regardless of whether or not they were ready to live on their own. Most were not, but it was common practice for group homes to give young people a subway token on their birthday and directions to Covenant House. That's what happened to Tony.

Not that he minded very much. He had spent the last several years in that group home beginning the pursuit of his childhood dream: becoming a big time drug dealer and gangster.

"I watched television shows and movies in the '70s that glorified drug dealers," he tells me now. "I saw the same thing in the Harlem projects. The gangster was the one with the money, the cars, the nice clothes and the women. The gangster was popular and could get into the best nightclubs, and that's what I wanted. Most kids grow up hoping to become a firefighter, police officer, or sports star. I knew early on I wanted to be a drug dealer, and I put all my energies into that. School meant nothing to me because I knew I didn't need an education to be a gangster."

But even aspiring gangsters need a place to sleep at night, hence his need for Covenant House.

After being tossed out of Covenant House, Tony lived in some of the cavernous eight hundred-bed shelters operated by the City of New York. They were frightening, dangerous places in the 1980s, and I once asked Tony if he was ever afraid.

"Not really," he responded. "I saw the shelters as just another place I could sell drugs from. And I worked during the day as 'security' in a whorehouse. I learned how to handle myself."

Tony started out in his own mind as a dealer of drugs first, and as a user second. But the roles began to switch after a few years. "I found myself using more and more—crack cocaine, freebasing, angel dust, anything I could get my hands on. All drug users talk about 'hitting the bell.' For example, the first time I freebased cocaine I reached this incredible high. That's hitting the bell. So you want to get that high again, but for some reason the next time you freebase, you get high, but not the intense type of high you got that first time. But you want that unbelievable feeling, so you keep using more and more in an effort to hit the bell. But you can't, it's impossible. So you get trapped trying.

"Every few years I'd check into a thirty-day detox to try to get clean, but it never worked. I'd leave the rehab and go right back to dealing and using. And then I got arrested."

When Tony was released after two years in jail he called me, and we got together for coffee. He looked much older than when I'd last seen him; two years in prison ages a person much faster than two years in freedom. We talked about everything, and he insisted, "I'm going straight. I'm telling you, I'm never going back to jail." But less than a year later he did, this time on a robbery charge, with a sentence of two to four years. In one of his letters to me he admitted he was robbing someone as part of a drug deal. As the 1980s ended it was sad but true that Tony had spent almost half of the decade incarcerated.

Tony was released after two years in jail and was never arrested again. He told me that of the guys he hung out with, almost all were now dead or serving very long sentences. He'd had enough of that. He earned a living at minimum wage jobs. Every few months we'd arrange to meet for pizza at Ray's Famous on 8th Avenue and 46th Street. We'd eat, laugh, tell stories, and take in a movie. Once we saw *Stargate* and as we exited the theater Tony spotted a sidewalk photographer who charged $5 for an instant 4 x 6 photo. "Come on, Mark, I want a photo of us." We put our arms around each other's shoulders as the guy took the shot. Tony paid him, and then I pulled out a five and insisted on a second shot so I could have one too. So we did it again. As I walked Tony to the subway he said, "This is the first time in ages I had fun without using drugs."

I knew from that sad statement that drugs were still a part of Tony's life. In fact, for the number of times that Tony met me at Ray's Famous there were just as many times when he failed to show. I'd sit in that pizzeria waiting, waiting, waiting, sometimes with my young son Aiden, but no Tony. One time we scheduled a 6:00 P.M. rendezvous and I called him at 5:00 P.M. to make sure he was going. "I'll definitely be there," he insisted. But he didn't show up. He would always call me a few weeks later with an excuse, which I always pretended to believe, but I knew the real reason: Tony was still using drugs. He might not be dealing, but he was definitely using. And when someone is a drug addict, nothing is more important than getting high, including friends.

There were many times I felt like giving up on Tony. But I made the commitment to him, I didn't give up on him, and now I am very glad I didn't because today he is drug-free. How do I know? For one thing, he actually shows up when he's supposed to meet me. And he looks and sounds better. In fact, as I write this it is the very day of his four-year anniversary of sobriety.

(I took him out for lunch to celebrate, at Yolanda's Restaurant on 149th Street in the Bronx; we've moved up from Ray's Famous.) He has an apartment and a full-time job as a plumber's apprentice. He had a baby nearly five years ago. Tony had her baptized and I am her godfather.

When I asked him what made him finally change, give up the drugs, the dealing, the crime, and the self-destructive behavior, he answered, "There was a woman I used to smoke crack with, and I used to laugh at her because she'd point to a wall and swear that she saw people coming out of the wall. Then one day I started seeing people come out of that wall. It scared the hell out of me. I was becoming like the people I once laughed at and made fun of. The drugs were making me lose touch with reality. And I was tired of getting high. I was tired of giving my money away to some dealer. I could see that I was living for drugs. I was working only so I could have money to buy drugs. So I called this friend of mine who I used to get high with, but he had stopped a few years earlier. He frequently told me, 'There is a better way to live. Call me when you are ready to stop using.' I called him and told him I was ready. He took me to a hospital and checked me in for a seven-day detox. But the difference this time was that as soon as I got out of that hospital my friend was there and drove me straight to a Narcotics Anonymous (NA) meeting.

"NA gave me my life back. When I started making meetings I knew it would work. It had to. If it didn't, I knew I was going to die soon.

"NA brings you back to normal society. The people there give you the support you need to stay straight. It teaches you that if you have a Higher Power in your life, you will not use drugs again. I know now that God has a plan for everyone, and mine is to do as much as I can to help as many people as possible. I know now that God wants us to be happy, and that happiness means having a roof over your head, food in your stomach, and being able to take care of your family. NA taught me all that."

One of the NA principles is that a member must share the good news of recovery with others. So over the years I have asked Tony to meet with the teenagers I work with now. These kids may not be addicts, but I know most of them use drugs and alcohol and are at high risk for addiction in the future. Tony is incredibly effective with these young people. He knows exactly where they are coming from, what their families are like, their neighborhoods, and what's going on in their heads. His message is straight, from-the-street, and not complicated: "I was once like you. I thought I was invincible. I thought I could do and sell drugs and make a lot of easy money. It doesn't work that way. Most of the people I did it with are dead or doing time. I'm lucky to even be here today. You think your drug pals are your friends. They are not. Mark and the other counselors here are your real friends. Listen to them. Stay away from drugs. Stay in school and get an education. That's the way to a happy life. Don't make the mistakes I made."

I've known Tony twenty-two years now. His recovery from addiction and from a life of self-destruction is truly amazing, a testament to God's power to turn people's lives around no matter how dark their past may have been. I feel privileged to have been part of his life, but believe me, there were at least fifty times during those two decades when I felt like bailing out on him. Being stood up in a pizza parlor in Manhattan for the umpteenth time, finding out he was fired from yet another job, watching him go back to jail for a repeat drug-related offense—all this was extremely frustrating. Many times it occurred to me that I had plenty else to do in my life other than try to help Tony.

But for some reason I hung in there with him. Why, I am not even sure. It's just that every time he turned to me for help, I decided to forget the mistakes he had made in the past and assist him in whatever way I could. Most of the time that meant just being his friend, somebody who would listen to him, somebody he could trust.

I think God brought Tony into my life to remind me of how he never gives up on any of us. When we turn to God, he too forgets the mistakes we've made in the past. The slate is wiped clean. He listens to us as a friend, comforts us and welcomes us with compassion and love.

As God is with us, so we should be with the young people in our lives.

Role Model

Young people in our society need positive role models. Desperately. There are already plenty of negative ones for them to follow. Young people have a need to be *shown,* through flesh and blood action, how to live in a positive, life-enhancing way. Parents should be the primary positive role model, but youth ministers, pastors, coaches, mentors, teachers, aunts, uncles, grandparents, employers, and others can also serve as positive role models. Adults have to walk the talk. Too many times I have encountered a parent who bemoans the fact that a daughter is using drugs, yet I know that the parent is a drug user or abuses alcohol. The daughter knows it, so the parent's plea to her to stay off drugs is ignored. I've seen a parent shed tears over a son's penchant for violent behavior, for engaging in frequent fights at school, only to later find out that there is a history of domestic violence in the house, or that the father thinks that by belting his son around he will effect some positive change in him. I've heard a parent express frustration that her daughter uses foul language, yet the parent curses. A mother is terrified that her daughter will contact AIDS because of her promiscuous behavior, yet the mother becomes involved in inappropriate relationships that are no secret to her daughter.

Some people believe athletes, celebrities, and political leaders should be the role models for their youth. Forget it. Turn to the sports pages of any newspaper and you are likely to read about some athlete who has been arrested for drug abuse, domestic violence, or is refusing to play this season because he thinks he should be earning $6 million a year instead of $5 million. Turn on MTV or E! for an hour and you will see twenty very poor role models for youth. And it is the rare political leader whom you would want to serve as a role model for your child.

You must be the role model for your child. I was lucky. I had parents who were role models for me. I watched how they treated people. I listened to how they spoke to others. I learned respect from them, honesty, and keeping my word. I can still remember being in church with my family when a young man a few pews in front of us fainted and hit the ground. My father was the one to emerge from the crowd, pick him up, and care for him. That showed me how to respond to others in need, even if a stranger. I can remember, while only in first grade, being bullied by some older kids around the corner when walking home from school. My mother was the one to come to my rescue and confront them. That's how I learned about standing up for those who are weak and unable to stand up for themselves. I had an uncle who, when his neighbor died suddenly, took care of the man's family financially and in every other way for the next twenty years, until the kids were grown up. They thank him to this day. I saw him do that. It left a strong impression on me, teaching me to, in biblical terms, "comfort the widow and orphan." I had a pastor to look up to who, when he arrived at our parish, didn't let dwindling numbers at Sunday services discourage him. He got people excited about being part of a parish again. He challenged them to participate and build up the church. They responded, in droves. He taught me that attitude means everything, that you can take an organization that was in decline and make it great again. He too was a role model for me.

I didn't have to rely on sports stars and politicians to be my role models. I had many excellent ones right in my life. And when I started working with homeless and runaway youth, the most improbable and unlikely one of all came along to guide me. Her name was Marge.

I first met her in 1980. I was only twenty-three, one year out of Villanova University, and working for a large insurance company on Madison Avenue as a management trainee. I lived on the upper east side of Manhattan and was a yuppie before the term was even invented. Everything was right out there in front of me for the taking in terms of material and financial success. But I could not quell this nagging sense that I was supposed to be doing something different with my life, something to do with helping the poor. I didn't know where this sense was coming from, but it was strong. Even now it is hard to put into words, but it was almost an instinct, a deep gnawing at the heart and mind, a call.

I didn't tell too many of my friends about this, but I did tell one fellow Villanova graduate who still lived near the university. She called me one day to tell me about a volunteer fair the school would be hosting during an upcoming Saturday. Representatives from different helping organizations were scheduled to be there to talk about full-time volunteer opportunities. They included, among others, the Maryknoll Lay Missioners, the Peace Corps, VISTA, and the Jesuit Volunteer Corps.

I drove to Villanova that Saturday in October and when I arrived at the event I noticed that Covenant House was represented. I had heard of Covenant House, and in fact a friend of mine worked there. I knew it was a shelter for homeless and runaway teenagers, located in Times Square. A Franciscan priest, Fr. Bruce Ritter, ran it.

I listened that day to a number of presenters, and then it was Covenant House's turn. A thin, white-haired woman with thick large round glasses went to the front of the room. She looked to me to be in her mid-sixties.

"My name is Marge Crawford," she said, "and I am a member of the Covenant House Faith Community. We make a one-year commitment to live in community and work with homeless and runaway teenagers. We receive $12 per week, and we pray for three hours every day. I am going to show you a film now, and then I will speak some more."

She sat down and the film came on. It ran for only twenty-five minutes, but it was very powerful. It showed graphic scenes of young people working as prostitutes in Times Square, and Covenant House's efforts to reach out and help them. You could not watch that film and help but be moved by the scenes of desperation and horror endured by so many young people. Fr. Ritter spoke of how he started Covenant House in the 1970s, and there were several scenes showing life in the faith community. When the film ended, Marge Crawford returned to the podium. In a quiet, undramatic way she told us what her life was like: starting each day at 7:00 A.M. with an hour of prayer with others in the faith community; eight to ten hours caring for young people who were homeless, lost, into drugs, or into prostitution; evening Mass at 5:30 P.M.; a communal dinner; 9:00 P.M. night prayer. She described some of the members of the faith community, which included young people right out of college as well as retirees. There were lawyers, doctors, social workers, nurses, teachers, a nun, and a priest. "We are committed to a simple life of prayer, community, and service to the poor," she told us. She made it sound incredibly appealing.

I went up to her afterward to tell her I was interested in visiting Covenant House, in particular the faith community. She gave me her phone number, and I promised to contact her.

I returned to Manhattan and called Marge a few days later. We picked a date to meet and she promised me a tour of Covenant House followed by dinner with the faith community.

When the day arrived, I left my Madison Avenue office early, at 4:00 P.M., and took a cab across the city. I got stuck in traffic, arriving at Covenant House half an hour later than I promised Marge I would be there. I was escorted to her office. Seeing her again, it occurred to me that she looked like every suburban grandmother I had ever known. Because I arrived late, she was in a rush to go over to the faith community for Mass. "No time for a tour now," she said, "but I have my calendar here. If you want to join the faith community you must first come on orientation for a week. Hmm, I see I have a spot open for the second week in May. Why don't I put you down?"

Now the whole time this is going on, I'm thinking, "Whoa, whoa, whoa, lady! Wait a minute! What you are doing? I'm just *thinking* about doing something like this. I haven't made up my mind yet!" And it was true. I mean, while I wasn't happy in the business world and felt this vague sense of being called to do something else, I wasn't quite ready to chuck it all for this. Maybe in a few years, but not right now.

"So the second week in May?" she said.

"Uhmm, yeah, put me down for the second week in May," I replied, but in my mind I was calming myself down, thinking, "That's six months away. That gives me plenty of time to back out."

We went over to the faith community for Mass and supper. I enjoyed meeting the people there. She had described them pretty well. Greg Loken was a young lawyer who had graduated from Harvard University and Law School, worked for a firm in Denver, and was now putting his education and training to use in youth advocacy. Gerry Stuhlman was two years out of the University of Connecticut and worked as a counselor with the older boys at Covenant House. Brenda Moscarella was a woman in her fifties, divorced and with a grown son; she was a counselor with the teenage mothers who arrived at Covenant

House with babies. There were about forty members of the faith community, and they didn't appear to be holy rollers or religious fanatics. They seemed like average people just trying to do something good with their lives. When supper ended a bunch of the guys walked down 8th Avenue to see the Knicks play in the Garden, and I walked with them.

Shortly afterward I started volunteering at Covenant House one night a week after work. I served snacks to the kids and played hoops with them in the gym. It didn't take me too long to realize that this was exactly what I wanted to be doing with my life. Soon I began to understand that I was being called to Covenant House now, not later on in my life. The more I prayed for God to guide me, the more my desire for a business career waned. Soon I was calling Marge with a different request: "Are there any orientation openings before May?"

She said there were. I attended a March orientation, resigned from my corporate job two months later, and joined the faith community on June 20, 1981. I made a one-year commitment but ended up staying almost three. During that time, Marge became a mentor, role model, and one of my closest friends. When I was down, when something a kid had said or done discouraged me and made me wonder why I was even there, she was the one who would get me out of my funk. It was like having your own Mother Teresa around. "God calls us to faithfulness, not to success....Our role is to love, not to judge....Just because a person does not rise to the standards we set doesn't mean that either we or they have failed." She was just the person I needed during that stretch of my life.

She influenced me in other ways. I had always been an upper-middle-class conservative, but the more I worked with homeless kids the more I began to question the economic and social forces that led to so much poverty and despair. Talking about this with Marge one day, she invited me to what she called "a little gathering for peace." A few days later I found myself standing in front of a nuclear weapons research lab holding a sign reading, "You can't hug a child with nuclear arms." This was in midtown Manhattan, and I was absolutely petrified that one of my former business peers would walk by and see me. I wondered on what kind of journey Marge was leading me.

It turned out to be a good one. Marge continued to invite me to peace marches, retreats, and liturgies. She introduced me to Fr. Daniel Berrigan, the famed antiwar priest from the 1960s who I discovered was still alive and well (and protesting) in the 1980s. She handed me books that made a strong case for the connection between military spending and poverty. And she had no fear about being arrested for her actions. One autumn she protested in front of the Capitol in Washington, D.C. The Reagan administration was funding death squads in El Salvador and other South American countries, nuns and priests were dying, and Marge was part of the Catholic peace movement that was determined to speak out against this. She ended up spending five days in a D.C. jail. "How was it?" I asked her when she returned. "Great," she replied. "I taught the prostitutes in there how to say the Rosary."

Everything she did was made even more remarkable when I discovered her background and history. Marge, it turned out, was from a prominent upstate New York family. Her late husband had been a State Supreme Court justice. Many of the judges who were now sentencing her had once known and even clerked under him. Marge's family was wealthy, and she had raised a family of several children. The last thing most widows in her position would have done was give up a relaxing retirement to move into a shelter for homeless youth in a decayed Times Square and work for practically nothing.

I left Covenant House and the faith community in 1983 to pursue graduate studies. Marge's health began to falter at that time. She had problems with her kidneys and started dialysis. But her spirits were as up as ever. I'd occasionally meet her for lunch at a restaurant in Times Square. "Want to order a drink?" she'd ask. "No, Marge, I don't like to drink during the day," I'd respond. "Well, I'm having a Bloody Mary," she'd say and then giggle. And she'd order one.

Our contact continued like this for years, but toward the late 1980s she became more frail and had less energy. At one point she fell and broke her hip. Then she was diagnosed with a brain tumor. Those of us who knew and loved her prepared ourselves mentally for her departure, but miraculously she overcame even that. In 1990, Marge was diagnosed with cancer. She still lived in a private room in the faith community but with full-time nursing care. She began to deteriorate rapidly and was in a lot of pain.

One evening I received a phone call from one of Marge's closest friends. She told me that Marge had decided to discontinue her dialysis treatment. She had talked to a priest and he had assured her that her decision was acceptable in the eyes of God and the Church. Marge was a devout Catholic who would never have done anything of which the Church disapproved. "Marge is asking that all her friends come and visit her," I was told.

So I went two days later, during the evening. It felt funny being back in the building where I had lived for almost three years. Marge was the only person still there from my time; everyone else, like me, had moved on to other pursuits. I found my way to her room. There were about half a dozen other people already in there, so I had to wait. After about half an hour it was my turn to see her.

She was lying down in a hospital bed, pillows propped up under her head. She tilted her head to see me, and smiled. I thought of the first time I met her and how lively she had been, and how tired she looked now. But even so, she seemed incredibly at peace. She looked tired, but not worried or anxious in any way.

"Hi, Marge."

"Mark, I'm glad you came. It's so good to see you."

"I'm glad too. How are you feeling?"

"Oh, I've been better," she laughed. "But I'm okay, I'm really okay. Tell me about yourself. Tell me what you're doing these days."

I told her about my work with homeless kids, that I had recently been named director of a shelter in Brooklyn. I told her what the kids were like and how some of them reminded me of the kids we had known ten years earlier.

"That's great, I'm so glad to hear that you're still doing God's work," she said.

"Well don't forget, you got me started in this racket."

She laughed again. "Don't blame me! I think it had more to do with the Holy Spirit than with me."

We talked for a few minutes more, but there was still quite a crowd waiting to see her. I said goodbye, and I did it quickly, because I could feel the tears welling up inside.

About three days later the call came from that same friend. "Marge passed away last night. She wasn't in any pain. A priest was at her side and administered the sacraments."

If anyone deserved a 5th Avenue funeral and all the accoutrements that come with it, it was Marge. After all, she was the widow of a judge and from a prominent family. But that wouldn't have been her at all. Instead she had requested a funeral ceremony in the chapel of the Covenant House faith community, a place in which she had prayed for literally thousands of hours. Hundreds of former community members showed up along with her family and other friends. Marge's casket was a simple unvarnished pine box. I'm sure she specified that. At a certain point in the ceremony people were asked to share their most fond memories of Marge. Person after person attested to her faith, how she helped people, and how she brought people to a clearer and deeper understanding of God's love.

The ceremony ended and the casket was wheeled out of the chapel onto the very street where Marge had ministered to homeless youth. A saxophone player did a slow and soft version of "When the Saints Go Marching In."

"Where did they get him?" I asked someone.

"Marge's son hired him," I was told. I knew Marge's son; he was a well-known illustrator who had visited the community many times.

"Where'd you find the sax player?" I asked him.

"I took the subway here this morning and heard him playing on the platform," he answered, "and I offered him $40 to come in here to play for my mother's funeral."

I just cracked up when I heard that.

"Marge must have absolutely loved it," I told him.

"I'm sure she did," he replied.

Taking It Seriously

Working with and counseling adolescents is serious work. Human lives are at stake. It is not factory work. It is not a business. Surgeons have to take their work very seriously; if they make a mistake, permanent damage to a human being could be the result, perhaps even the loss of a life. Parents and those of us who work with young people must regard our interactions with them in the same way. We have to be vigilant in how we speak to, and in front of, our youth. We must constantly be aware of our actions and our choices, cognizant of the reality that we are having an effect, for good or ill, on our children. We must keep in mind the possibility that we can be the one person who makes the crucial difference in a teenager's life, who is able to reach a youth who is in distress and make an impact on him or her.

After only six weeks at Covenant House as a counselor, Fr. Ritter asked me to serve in the position known as ombudsman. It was a strange title for a strange job. Fr. Ritter rarely had time to even drop in at the shelter. The great majority of his time was spent fundraising and giving speeches. There was a Franciscan nun in charge of the shelter, but Fr. Ritter insisted on having a member of the faith community serve as his eyes and ears to inform him of the goings-on there. This person was to report directly to him, providing him with an honest and frank appraisal of the shelter and if it was meeting the standards he expected. As one board member described the job, "You are essentially Fr. Bruce's CIA." The standard Fr. Ritter most valued was that of "open intake," which meant that no child in need be turned away, no matter how full the shelter may be.

Once I became ombudsman, I quickly learned there was more to the job than reporting facts to Fr. Ritter. Every child being discharged from Covenant House had the right to appeal that discharge if he thought it was unfair. Kids were discharged from Covenant House every day for a variety of reasons—lying to staff, cursing them out, fighting, using or dealing drugs in the shelter, carrying a weapon, and failure to make a serious effort to look for work. But Fr. Ritter was a strong believer in mercy. He constantly preached that people should be forgiven for what they did wrong, especially kids. And he wanted the ombudsman to exemplify that.

When kids came to me, I'd have to work hard on researching their case, talking to counselors, and going through the youth's file. Many times I felt like I was between a rock and a hard place. These were the times when the facts were in dispute, when it wasn't clear if staff were being fair, when the possibility existed that a kid really was being treated unjustly, or when the past reputation of a young person shadowed a genuine change of heart on his or her part. I would be faced with the decision whether or not to let this young person stay at Covenant House. These were difficult and often lonely moments.

One night, a dozen kids poured out of the front doors of Covenant House, separated into two opposing groups, and proceeded to beat the hell out of each other. Staff eventually broke things up. There were strict rules against fighting, and any kids who violated those rules were to be discharged immediately. At 9:00 P.M. all twelve were ordered out of the shelter, unable to return for thirty days.

The next morning, one of them showed up at my office. He was a tall, lanky, African American, age seventeen. I can't even remember his name. He walked in slowly. I invited him to sit down. His nose was covered in bandages.

"What happened to you?" I asked him.

"I was in that fight last night and someone cold-cocked me and broke my nose," he replied.

"Why were you fighting?" I asked him.

"I wasn't, I swear to God I wasn't," he said. "I went out there to try to break it up, but the next thing I knew I was hit in the face and there was blood all over me. I made it down to St. Vincent's Hospital and they took care of me."

"Did you sleep there?" I asked.

"No," he said, "they wouldn't let me. I came back here to Covenant House in the middle of the night but they told me that Fr. Ritter had ordered everyone discharged who was in the fight."

I found out later that this was true. Fr. Ritter had been driving by, saw the scene, and ordered the staff to discharge the kids.

"So where did you sleep?" I asked.

"Out on the streets."

"Where will you stay tonight?" I asked.

"I don't know."

"Can you stay with family, with relatives?"

"No," he answered. "That's why I came to see you. I want to stay here. I have nowhere else to go."

At that moment I watched little drops of blood leak from his bandaged nose and fall onto my desk.

"I'm sorry," he said, wiping them off with his shirtsleeve.

"That's alright," I said, and I suddenly felt tremendous pity for this young man. Watching blood dripping out of him, and he apologizing for it and wiping it off with his sleeve—it just all seemed so incredibly sad and unfair.

I asked him to wait outside my office for a minute. I then called his counselors. While they couldn't vouch for his conduct at the melee, they did verify that he was a model resident with a good chance of finding a job and moving into an independent living situation. They had no problem with his returning, in fact they recommended it. They confirmed that he had no other place to stay.

I really wanted to let this kid back in, but I feared it would open the doors to the other eleven kids who were in the fight, all of whom could claim to have been innocent bystanders as well. Where would I draw the line as to whom to admit and whom to reject? And I wasn't exactly comfortable overturning Fr. Ritter's decision, who was now out of town and beyond reach.

I called St. Mark's, an emergency youth residence in the Greenwich Village section of Manhattan. I was never so appreciative of my sales training from my previous employer, an insurance company, as I convinced the director there to take this young man in.

I asked him to step back into my office. He did and sat down across from me.

"I can't let you back into Covenant House," I said, "but I did find you a spot at St. Mark's."

"Thank you. Thank you very much," he said.

We shook hands and he left.

So I got lucky. I found this young man a place to go to, but what if the director of St. Mark's had said no? What if he had no room? What would I have done? What was the right thing to do in that situation?

For the first time it really hit me. Working with young people was serious business. This wasn't about selling insurance any more. This was about human lives. It was the real thing.

Forgiveness

One of the main tenets of the Christian faith is forgiveness. "Forgive us our trespasses as we forgive those who trespass against us." The Prodigal Son. The Good Shepherd who goes after the lost sheep. Meister Eckhart, the thirteenth-century German mystic, frequently wrote about forgiveness—"If God now finds a person ready to be different, He will have no regard for what he used to be. God is a God of the present. He takes you and receives you as He finds you—not what you have been, but what you are now. Sins vanish into God's abyss, faster than it takes me to shut my eyes, and so they become utterly nothing, as if they had never happened...."

If youngsters do something wrong, forgive them for it. If they follow a path you believe is incorrect, and later realize this, don't remind them of the mistakes made. Let it go. Treat them the way God treats us.

I left Covenant House and the faith community after serving there for twenty-eight months. I attended graduate school at New York University for two years, and then returned to working with homeless youth. I became assistant director at a small program called My Brother's Place. It was funded by a Catholic religious order, the Pallottine Fathers. We had three residences for homeless young men ages eighteen to twenty-four.

One of the homes was located on Willis Avenue in the Mott Haven section of the South Bronx. This was during the height of the crack epidemic that ravaged many neighborhoods of New York City during the mid-1980s. Drug dealing was rampant in Mott Haven, and the homicide rate was astronomical. It was not a good location for a group home, but My Brother's Place did not have the money to relocate to a safer neighborhood, and there was no shortage of homeless young men looking for a place to live. So we did our best to run the home in as safe a manner as possible.

I was at My Brother's Place for almost a year when Santos arrived. He was nineteen years old and originally from Puerto Rico. He came to the United States when he was sixteen, absolutely alone, with no family or relatives here to welcome him and take him in. He lived on the streets, spent some time at Covenant House, and then came to My Brother's Place. He was a very nice young man, a gentle person, but it didn't take us long to figure out he was using crack. We offered to get him into a drug treatment program, but he refused. He insisted he could get off drugs on his own, but we could see this wasn't working. He would frequently stay out past curfew, and when he did come in he was usually high. At a staff meeting in late January 1987 we all agreed we had no choice but to ask him to leave.

We decided that we would ask him to leave that Saturday. I called up to the Mott Haven house that day and asked one of the counselors there how Santos had taken the news. I was told he took it well and did not protest, as if he knew it was coming. I hung up the phone and felt badly that we were not able to help Santos, but I also was pleased he left without any kind of scene.

The priest who ran My Brother's Place, Fr. Jim MacDonald, always allowed all former residents to come to the Bronx house on Sunday for Mass, followed by supper. Santos showed up that day, attended Mass, and ate. He approached Fr. MacDonald afterward, telling him he had nowhere to stay. Fr. MacDonald gave him $60 and directions to a YMCA where he could stay for a few nights. Santos then left, as did Fr. MacDonald.

There were three live-in counselors in that Bronx house. It was Super Bowl Sunday that day, and two of the counselors put eight of the twelve boys from the house in a van and headed over to our Brooklyn house for a Super Bowl party. That left four boys in the Bronx house and the one remaining staff member, Sr. Virginia Thomann.

Sr. Virginia had come to My Brother's Place as a full-time, live-in volunteer about six months earlier. She was from Pennsylvania, in her late sixties, thin and wiry, with gray hair. She described herself as a maverick nun; she had not lived with her religious community, the Sisters of the Good Shepherd, in years. She moved about on her own, working and living in different places, fulfilling a variety of ministries with the poor and marginalized. She read about My Brother's Place in a national Catholic newspaper, *Our Sunday Visitor,* and applied to join us. We accepted her right away. She didn't have much experience with street kids, but she had tremendous compassion and joy. When she arrived she was quickly able to reach out to and connect with them. She was also an organized person who was good with numbers, so we made her the business manager of the house.

That Sunday night, with most of the boys and staff now at the Brooklyn house, Sr. Virginia proceeded down to the basement office while the four remaining boys watched the Super Bowl upstairs. Sometime during the game Santos came back. He rang the front doorbell, and the boys let him in. The boys later told us it was obvious he was high. He apparently never made it to the YMCA, most likely using the $60 to purchase and smoke some crack. He sat and watched the game with the boys for a few minutes, then asked if any staff were around. They told him Sr. Virginia was in the basement office. He got up from his chair and headed in that direction.

About fifteen minutes later Santos reappeared in the living room, said a quick goodbye to the others, and left.

When the game ended one of the boys wanted to ask Sr. Virginia something, so he walked downstairs to the staff office where he knew she was. The door was closed. He knocked. No answer. He yelled for her. No response. He banged on the door. Nothing. He ran upstairs and asked the others to come down. They too tried but with the same results. One of them ran up to her room on the third floor, thinking she had left the basement office. But she wasn't there either.

There was a window in the staff office, facing out onto the front sidewalk on Willis Avenue. The boys ran out of the house and to that window, peering inside. They banged on the window and yelled for Sr. Virginia, and then one of them saw her, slumped over the desk, a pool of blood beneath her.

The boys ran back inside and called the police. A car arrived within minutes. The police broke into the office and found Sr. Virginia dead from multiple stab wounds to the neck.

A few minutes later the boys and staff who had been at the Brooklyn Super Bowl party returned. One of the counselors called me at home.

It was just past midnight, and in this line of work, when the phone rings that late at night your heart skips a beat. Mine skipped that night, and then I gasped when I heard the words, "Mark, you'd better get up here. Sr. Virginia is dead. She was murdered."

I immediately called Fr. MacDonald. Both of us lived in Brooklyn, so I picked him up in my car and we drove to the Bronx in the midst of a fierce snowstorm. When we pulled onto Willis Avenue we were faced with the sight of twenty to thirty police cars, all with their lights going. It was an unreal scene.

We walked up the front steps, and a policewoman met us at the door. She asked who we were, and we told her. I stood at the entrance to the living room, where all the boys and the staff sat together. They looked scared and confused. There were cops and detectives everywhere.

I asked the policewoman if all the boys who had been present in the house were accounted for. She told me yes, except for one: a young man named Santos. He was missing.

The boys and staff eventually went to bed, and the police carried away Sr. Virginia's body. Fr. MacDonald and I stayed for a few hours, then headed back to Brooklyn in the early hours of the morning. We were both exhausted. Neither of us could believe what had happened. People who do this kind of work always know that it is possible, that a kid could kill a counselor, but it is a fear you learn to live with but hope never happens, the same kind of fear a police officer or firefighter lives with every day. But this time it did happen. The worst happened.

The police warned us that they would be letting the press know about the murder and that we should expect to be besieged. We were. Every major New York City newspaper had it on the front page, and the sleazier ones put it in headlines such as "Nun Killer on the Loose." The papers and all the television networks were at our door, trying to interview staff and even kids. We held to a tight "no comment" policy, only later granting interviews.

Santos was still at large, and the police were feverishly looking for him. Newspapers and news shows asked people to turn him in. A few days later he showed up at his job to collect his paycheck, and the police were there waiting for him. His capture was front-page news, with pictures of him in cuffs in the back seat of a police cruiser splashed across the city's dailies.

The week ended with Cardinal O'Connor saying a memorial Mass for Sr. Virginia in the church around the corner from the Bronx house.

Santos was placed in Rikers Island prison awaiting trial. I went to visit him. I didn't really know Santos that well. I had probably had only one or two conversations with him during his brief stay at My Brother's Place. I'm not even sure why I went to see him, except that I always took to heart Jesus' words, "And when I was in prison you visited me."

They had Santos in an isolation cell. As the saying goes, there is honor among thieves, and Santos was likely to be killed himself if placed in the general population, considering the crime he was charged with. He was glad to see me, and I asked him how he was, how he felt, and what the conditions were like. I asked him if his family had been by to see him, and he reminded me that his entire family was in Puerto Rico.

Eventually I asked Santos the question, "Did you do it? Did you kill Sr. Virginia?"

He looked directly at me.

"I don't know. Maybe I did. I really don't know. The only thing I know is that I smoked crack that night, and I was so high I can't even remember what happened."

I believed Santos then, and I still believe him. I believe he took that $60 from Fr. MacDonald, smoked it up, and God knows what he did from that point on. I have heard of other instances when people were so high on crack that they committed murder and never even remembered doing it. This is probably what happened with Santos.

About a year later a trial was held and, as I expected, Santos was convicted of murder. He received a sentence of fifteen to twenty-five years and sent upstate. I found out where he was placed and began writing to him. Once or twice a year I'd send him a letter, and he would write back.

An entire decade passed. And then, in the summer of 1996 I went on vacation with my son to upstate New York. One day, while driving to a Dairy Queen a few towns away from where we were staying, we passed a sign with the words, "Cayuga Correctional Facility."

"Why does that sound familiar?" I wondered.

When we returned to our rented vacation house, I took out my address book and turned to Santos's entry. Yes, that is why Cayuga Correctional sounded familiar. It was his prison.

So I decided to visit him. Just like ten years earlier, I wasn't exactly sure why. It just seemed like the right thing to do.

I put off seeing Santos until the last day of my two-week vacation. I knew I would go, but I felt strange. It had been so many years since his crime, and since I had last seen him at Rikers. I wondered how he would react to my unannounced visit, and what we would talk about.

When I arrived at Cayuga Correctional I signed in at the prison entrance, emptied all my pockets and went through the prison rituals I know so well. I waited while they summoned Santos. When he walked in he was shocked to see me. He came right over, shook my hand, smiled, and we embraced. I was surprised by how much older he looked. No longer the teenager I knew, he was almost thirty, an adult, and going prematurely bald. Genetics, I wondered, or the result of ten years of prison life?

I was not sure what to talk about, and neither was he, so I brought up the names of the various staff members from My Brother's Place. We traded stories about them and about the kids who were there. Most of the stories were funny, and I discovered that prison had not diminished his sense of humor.

I asked Santos who had come to visit him during the last ten years. "You are the first," he told me, explaining that while his sister had emigrated from Puerto Rico to the United States, she had not managed to make the trek north to see him.

Santos then brought up the issue of parole. This was in 1996, and he told me his first parole hearing would be in 2001. It struck me how he talked about 2001 like most people would talk about October when it is September. I wondered how someone could hold on to hope for that long, especially knowing it is a dim hope. Chances are that a person convicted of killing a nun will not be paroled at the first opportunity.

How did Santos get up each day and go about his prison business? What motivated him? What kept him from plunging into a deep, dark depression? I was tempted to ask him, but I did not. He was somehow functioning in that prison, and I did not want to set off the mental dominos that would take him off that course.

We continued with our small talk until the corrections officer in charge of the visiting area told us our hour was up. I was half-relieved. My ten-year-old son was waiting for me back at our cabin, probably anxious to go fishing. And I felt awkward with Santos. I realized now that written correspondence was easier than face to face. We hugged each other goodbye, and I encouraged him to hang in there.

We continued our correspondence. Santos asked me to mail him certain books, some of them about Hatha Yoga. He also wrote that he was taking a painting class in prison but the supplies were inadequate. I asked him what specific materials he would like, and he wrote back with a detailed list of brushes, paints, and paper. I ordered them through the Internet and sent them to him. A few months later he wrote asking for a subscription to a magazine that would have many landscape pictures, so I subscribed to *Down East* and *American Artist* for him.

Shortly afterward I began receiving some stunning artwork in the mail from Santos. I had sent him a Polaroid shot of my son that was part of our family Christmas card. Santos sent me a framed pencil drawing of this picture that was an incredible likeness. Other paintings arrived every few months, and when I was remarried in May 2001, a strikingly beautiful seaside landscape painting arrived days before as a wedding gift. My wife framed it and it hangs prominently in our living room.

As expected, Santos was denied parole in 2001. He will have another opportunity to apply in two years. He is now in a prison about two hours north of New York City. My wife, sons, and I go to visit him at least once a year, usually around Christmas. He loves to ask my son Aiden questions about school, sports, and music. Santos's sister now lives in Westchester County, New York, and visits him regularly with her two daughters, so at least he now has family coming to see him. Santos completed his high school equivalency while in jail and was taking college courses in pursuit of a bachelor's degree, but Gov. Pataki cancelled the program. My wife and I established a foundation to raise money for Santos to take correspondence courses from Ohio University; we know that without a bachelor's degree, his chances of supporting himself outside the prison walls are very slim. And when I ask him where he thinks he will live when he does get out, he replies that his sister's place is too small, and he has no other family members or friends with whom he can stay. I once asked the prison social work staff what help they offer inmates in terms of finding housing when they leave. The answer was not encouraging: "We give them a listing of the homeless shelters in the city."

I do not share my fears and concerns with Santos. He has enough on his mind just to stay sane and healthy in jail for the next few years. When he gets out, whenever that may be, my wife and I will help him in whatever way we can.

There is a wonderful novel by Oscar Hijuelos called *Mr. Ives' Christmas*. Mr. Ives lives in Manhattan in the 1950s. He is a graphic artist, a devout Catholic, in a happy marriage, and he has a wonderful son he absolutely adores. The son is eighteen or nineteen years old and in a Catholic seminary studying to become a priest. He walks down a city street one evening when a young Hispanic man, for absolutely no reason at all, stabs and murders him. It is a terrible, terrible, unspeakable loss for Mr. Ives. His heart is just broken. His pain is excruciating and inevitably takes a toll on every aspect of his life—his marriage, his work, everything. The remainder of the book describes all this, but near the end he decides to visit the person who killed his son. It is twenty years after the murder, and the man has served his time and is living with his family in Spanish Harlem. Mr. Ives asks to see him not in order to accuse him or unleash upon him the agony he has felt due to the loss of his son. When they meet, it is a reconciliation. By this act Mr. Ives achieves a kind of peace.

I think of this book a lot when I think about Santos. I was as devastated as anyone when Sr. Virginia died. She was a sweet, caring woman who never deserved to die a cruel, violent death. She was my friend. There was much bitterness and anger in my heart toward Santos for what he did.

But feeding that bitterness and anger does not achieve internal peace. Forgiveness and reconciliation do. It was true for Mr. Ives. It's been true for me. It is what Jesus taught. It is what we all should live.

Honesty

Working with troubled young people, I have often been reminded of Jesus' instruction to his disciples, "You must be wise as serpents and gentle as doves." You will be of little use to adolescents if you let them manipulate and con you, and unfortunately, there are some who will do this. You have to be smart enough and strong enough to recognize such behavior, confront it, and not make excuses for it. Young people, although they may be angry for not getting their way, will ultimately respect you. And getting beyond this manipulation allows you the opportunity to get to the real issues in their life.

"Oh my God, everyone get up here—I've been robbed!"

I recognized the frantic voice immediately. It was Joe. He lived on the third floor of the Epiphany Youth Hostel in a large room with three other guys.

I was director of Epiphany. It was a renovated convent in the Williamsburg section of Brooklyn. We took in homeless young men ages sixteen to twenty-one. We had room for twenty of them, and we were almost always full. These were the kids who were too old for foster care, but who often had no real family to live with. We took in the kids who had nowhere to go. They'd come to us right out of jail or a drug rehab, or from nights sleeping on subways, under Grand Central Station, or on the streets. They could stay at Epiphany for a year, during which time we'd help them get their GED, find a job, and eventually an apartment. Epiphany was a good program. It really offered kids a leg up, a way out of poverty and homelessness.

Two other staff members and I tore up several flights of stairs to get to Joe's room. When we entered we saw it was trashed. Furniture was thrown around, locked closets had been broken into, and desk drawers were open, as if someone had been through them. And the window leading to the fire escape was wide open, indicating this had been the means of breaking in.

Joe was livid, screaming.

"They stole my stuff, they stole my stuff! Someone broke in here and look what they did. They even took my wallet out of my desk."

He started throwing furniture around, enraged. I watched him break a dresser drawer in anger. He kept screaming, "I can't believe this. This place isn't safe. Nothing is safe around here."

Joe was nineteen, a skinny white kid, in fact one of the few white kids ever to stay at Epiphany during my eighteen months there. He was estranged from his family; I did not know why. He had apparently bounced around a number of different institutions and came to the hostel from some short-term shelter where he'd been staying. He was always very friendly and respectful to me, but I knew he was nasty to most of the counselors. I was familiar with his type—he saw who had power and would cozy up to that person, while treating others with disdain.

Valentine Williams was a senior counselor and one of the staff members who ran up to Joe's room with me. Valentine worked two full-time jobs; one with us and one with the New York City Corrections Department. A middle-aged man originally from the island of Jamaica, he was nobody's fool. When he came upon the scene and witnessed Joe's tirade, he pulled me aside.

"This is suspicious, Mark. You mean to tell me someone from the outside climbed up that fire escape, in the front of the building, in broad daylight, and broke in here? I know there's crime in this neighborhood, but even thieves around here are not that cavalier. I think this has something to do with money we lent Joe recently."

Valentine explained that Joe had requested $40 about two weeks earlier to purchase prescription skin cream. Our office manager gave it to him on the condition that he produce a receipt, but he had yet to give her one. She kept asking for it, but Joe kept stalling her.

"I say we ask him right now for that receipt or at least proof that he purchased the cream," said Valentine.

I agreed to do it, but I doubted if Valentine was on the right track. Joe was just so furious about the break-in, it was hard for me to believe it was all an elaborate act. But Valentine went in and asked Joe for the receipts and the cream.

Joe shot right back: "The receipts were in my wallet, which was stolen."

"How about the skin cream?" asked Valentine.

Joe reached into his closet and pulled out a tube of some prescription cream, but most of the prescription label had been torn off.

"From which pharmacy did you purchase this?" asked Valentine.

"From my mother's. She works at a pharmacy, and I purchased it there," replied Joe.

I still didn't know what to make of all this, but Valentine continued to be suspicious, as was Nereida Colon, another of our counselors. Nereida was an immigrant from Ecuador who had been living in Brooklyn for several years. Even though she possessed only a high school diploma, she was an excellent counselor who had a way of cutting through all the nonsense street kids will sometimes throw at you. And she was able to connect with them on a real and deep level. Nereida went to our office, found Joe's file, located his mother's phone number in there, and called her. When she answered, Nereida asked her if she worked in a pharmacy.

"Yes, I do," she answered.

"Did Joe buy a tube of skin cream recently?" Nereida asked.

"No, he did not," she replied.

We had our answer.

Valentine, Nereida, and I asked Joe to come in to my office. We didn't even tell him that we had called his mother and what we had found out. Joe walked in, sat down, and Nereida just stared at him. It was beautiful, a work of art. She made the kid melt. She only had to ask one question: "What did you do with that money?"

Joe looked like he was about to launch into his alibi, but he didn't. He hesitated, then looked down at the ground, defeated.

"I gambled it away," he said.

Valentine had been right. This kid had staged his own burglary and then done a heck of an acting job. He had fooled me, and I was furious with him.

Joe asked if he could talk to Nereida alone. We let him. She told us later that he admitted he had a gambling addiction and wanted help. She promised him she would look for a program to help him with this, but he'd still have to pay us back the $40.

One would think that Joe would be rather contrite and cautious after pulling such a stunt. No way. Two days later we were rounding kids up for a house meeting on the second floor. Everyone was up there except Joe. Valentine found him on the pay phone, talking to his girlfriend. Valentine asked him politely to get off. "Sure," said Joe, who then ignored Valentine's request and stayed on the phone. A few minutes later Valentine asked him again, reminding him there was a mandatory house meeting starting upstairs. Joe gave the same response. Valentine returned a third time, and Joe started screaming at him: "Get away from me. Leave me alone. Get the hell out of here!" I was in the house meeting and heard all the commotion. I bolted from my seat and ran down the stairs. I saw Joe on the phone, Valentine confronting him, and Joe screaming up at me, "Mark, get him away from me. Get him away!" I stopped, pointed at Joe, and stated, "Get off that phone—now!" He did.

Joe went up to the community meeting and Valentine came over to me. He asked that Joe be suspended from Epiphany for two days.

"I need you to back me up on this, Mark. What he did the other day was outrageous, and now this. He needs to go, to cool his heels for a few days. Please." I didn't know if Joe had a place to go, but I felt it was important to support Valentine. Joe had committed a major faux pas two days earlier, we hadn't booted him out for that, and now he was back at it. He was really pressing us, and I agreed with Valentine that we needed to show him that he just could not continue to act like this without some serious consequences.

When the meeting ended we told Joe he'd have to leave for two days. He made some phone calls and found a relative on Long Island to take him in for the time being. He then left.

Valentine came to me the next day and thanked me for supporting him not only in suspending Joe, but for ordering him off the phone. "I felt like you really backed me up," he said. Counselors always live in fear that administrators will override their decisions, thereby eroding their authority and rendering them helpless to deal with acting-out kids. The longer I work in this field the more I realize how important it is to back staff up in their decisions. If the kids see staff as lacking authority, the staff is finished.

Sending Joe away for a few days was probably the best thing for him. When he returned, his attitude was greatly improved. The next day I received this letter from him.

Dear Mark,

I just wanted to apologize again. I realize what I did was wrong and I can't change it but I know how to correct it. I wish you can really understand what I'm going through. I went to a Gambler's Anonymous meeting yesterday and they told me what to do about changing my life around. Ever since I've been here I've put on a big front, and never expressed or talked about my real problems or feelings and that's how I screwed up. After I went to my meeting my girlfriend, me, and someone from the meeting sat down and I poured my heart out. They said I have to do it here at Epiphany. I really hope I can. I'm scared, I don't want to be discharged, and I don't want to go back to my old ways. What Nereida said to me the other day hit the spot. It brought back a lot of memories which I don't want because I don't think I can handle it again. All I'm asking is for a second chance. I promise I will find a job ASAP, I will go to Gambler's Anonymous meetings as much as possible, I will do extra chores and anything else you want. But please just give me a second chance. All I have in my life is you guys and my girlfriend and I don't want to lose it. I will do anything and everything to help myself, using you guys as my guide. Please try and understand.

Joe

P.S. Tonight I'm going to another meeting and maybe the guy I talked to will come and discuss what's going on with me to make you understand better.

Nereida Colon, the counselor who had gotten through to him a few days before, located a residential treatment program out on Long Island called South Oaks, specifically designed for gambling addicts. She even made all arrangements with Medicaid for him.

Joe went to the program, stayed a few months, during which time Nereida frequently visited him. When he left there, he found a job in a factory and got his own apartment.

We were able to help this young man because people like Valentine and Nereida would not allow themselves to be fooled. They confronted his manipulation, combining wisdom with compassion. That's what made the difference for Joe.

Faithfulness

Mother Teresa often said, "God calls us to faithfulness, not to success." I have had to take this message to heart many times when working with young people. Try as you might, you cannot be successful with every single one of them. It's impossible. There are some you try to help over and over again. You think that you are getting through to them. But internal or external forces can overwhelm kids like these, and they choose the wrong path.

You cannot take this personally, as if you have failed. There's a great line in the movie *Clean and Sober,* when Michael Keaton, playing a recovered cocaine addict, tries but cannot stop another addict from returning to drugs. Keaton feels as if he has failed and says to his Twelve-Step sponsor, "I should have been able to save her." And his sponsor replies, "Anyone in recovery knows it is impossible for one person to save another person. That is the greatest illusion of all. You do the best you can, but ultimately it is in the hands of the other person to save himself."

Wise words.

Doug Blancero ran a drop-in center for teenagers in Coney Island, Brooklyn, which was a very low-income and dangerous section of the city in the early 1990s. Doug worked with a lot of gang members, a quiet hero in New York City, in the same league as the police and firefighters—doing difficult and risk-filled work for little pay and no fanfare. He called me at Epiphany one day asking if I could help a seventeen-year-old named Hector.

"He's from Colombia," Doug told me, "and his parents were murdered a year ago in their home in some kind of drug dispute. Hector wasn't there at the time so he escaped, but he really has nowhere to live. He sleeps on a couch in our drop-in center once in a while. And I've noticed he's hanging out with some gang kids. I am very worried about him. He needs a place to stay and he needs some positive influences in his life."

I interviewed Hector and agreed to take him in. He was a little guy who spoke broken English. He was enrolled in a high school in Coney Island and traveled there by subway every morning. He was supposed to come right back to Epiphany afterward, but it rarely seemed to work out that way. He'd stroll in at all hours of the night, each time with a new excuse. We had a strict curfew at Epiphany, and I explained this to Hector. Then Doug started calling me with bad reports on Hector from his end of things: He wasn't attending school, he was involved in a break-in of a home, and he was spotted more and more with a gang.

When Hector began staying out all night and not even returning to Epiphany for days on end, we held a staff meeting and decided to discharge him. We told him, and the next day I received a letter from him.

Dear Mr. Mark,

I'm writing this letter to you because last night when I came inside the office, Mr. Chris the counselor told me that I was discharged for breaking the rules. Mr. Mark, you know that I'm not like all the kids that live at Epiphany. They do have a mother, father, and a roof to sleep under, but they have problems with their parents. My case is that if you discharge me, where am

*I going to sleep? I don't have a Mom or Dad. The only
people that I have is Doug Blancero and Epiphany. You
people have given me love, and I really appreciate it.*

*I know some of the things I've done are my fault,
but like I told you Mr. Mark, you're the only person
who can give me a chance. Please, you have to understand me. I don't want to go in the streets or the train.
Mr. Mark, I will be waiting for your answer.*
Sincerely,
Hector

We had a staff meeting that afternoon and I brought up the
issue of Hector's discharge.

"Can I first read you this letter?" I asked the staff. They
agreed.

I started reading it aloud to them but halfway through I
started to choke up. I handed it to another counselor to finish.

"Do you think we can give Hector another chance?" I
asked. They agreed to do so. One of the staff there gave Hector
the news that night. He was thrilled.

But less than a week later he was back at it—disappearing
for days at a time.

The lure of the street was just too strong.

We had to let him go.

Antoine was another kid who could have made it, should
have made it. He was a nineteen-year-old African American, the
rare young person who came to Epiphany with a high school
diploma under his belt. Not only that, he was enrolled as a
freshman in John Jay College in Manhattan. He attended
classes in the evening and looked for work by day. He was
proud of telling us that he was the only one from his family and
friends who was in college.

But you could see he was a kid who was really torn. On the
bulletin board in his bedroom were pictures of himself and his

friends from Queens. This was no college crowd. They had all the dress and gestures of drug dealing, gangs, and guns. Antoine clearly came from a gangster family and neighborhood. Part of him wanted to stay in college, get his degree, and succeed, but the pull of the street was very strong. Part of him wanted to be there.

Antoine stayed with us a few months, and we really worked hard to try to convince him that he could make it the legitimate, legal way. It was a losing battle though. He was rough on the counselors at Epiphany. He cursed out Nereida once, and the consequence for that was that he had to apologize to her at a house meeting. He did so, but then he threatened to hurt Valentine Williams. Valentine later went up to see him in his room, and Antoine cried his eyes out. He admitted how frustrated he was in college, how difficult the work was for him. He talked about the pressure on him from his friends and brothers to go back to his neighborhood and deal drugs.

We hoped that opening up to his feelings and frustrations like that would help Antoine stay the course at Epiphany, but it did not. His violence went from the verbal to the physical. He was mad at somebody one day and smashed the window in the door of his room. A few days later he was angry again and smashed the window in the kitchen door. We warned him that if this continued, he'd have to leave Epiphany.

Then he dropped out of college. We put him on full-time job search. His frustration level was very low by now, and I was there one afternoon when he was getting ready to go out for the afternoon. Somebody said something that ticked him off, and he smashed the glass case of the fire extinguisher as he walked out the door. I made an instantaneous decision: He had to leave Epiphany for good. I ran out after him and followed him down the street. It was cold and raining, and I didn't have a jacket on. I yelled after him to stop, that I wanted to talk with him. He ignored me and kept going, not even once turning around. Finally I yelled after him, "Antoine, you're discharged from the hostel." I went back and told the staff what I had said. No one disagreed with me.

That night we held our weekly house meeting, which took place at 9:00 P.M. When it ended a few kids went to sit out on the front steps for a smoke. That's when I heard several excited voices urging me to come out.

"Mark, get out here now! Your car—wait till you see it."

My heart was in my mouth. I ran out to find the windshield smashed. Broken glass was all over the front seat.

Several of the kids helped me clean out the glass on the seat, along with Chris Armstrong, one of our counselors.

"You're the guy making the tough decisions," he said, "and this is what can happen."

I drove back to the section of Brooklyn where I lived, peering through that part of the windshield that provided some visibility. I picked up my four-year-old son at his babysitter's house. He thought it was the greatest thing in the world to ride in a car with the air whipping right through the front. I just kept begging him not to tell his mother of this neat new experience.

I figured Antoine had done this. He knew when the house meeting would take place, with no one to stop him or witness the act. I had little doubt it was him when I arrived home and recognized his voice on my answering machine: "Don't come to work again. You're a dead man."

I did of course continue to go to work and never heard from nor saw Antoine again. I was angry about what he had done, but I felt even worse for the missed opportunities he would now lose in his life.

We had a similar situation with another youth named Titus. I can't remember how he ended up at Epiphany. He was a quiet young man, always respectful of staff and his peers. He was

African American, age nineteen, and in good physical shape. He was our quarterback the autumn we decided to start a flag football team at Epiphany. I always carried a beat-up football in the trunk of my car, and would occasionally take it out and toss it around on the street with some of the guys, but this fall we actually played other teams. Chris Armstrong coached a team in East New York, where he lived. They were our opponents most of the time. We usually lost, until Titus arrived. With his arm, we rarely lost.

Titus's goal was similar to most of the young men at Epiphany—find a job, go to school in the evenings, and eventually find an apartment. We helped Titus to find a minimum-wage job. He pursued a high school equivalency diploma in the evening. We thought he was well on the way to success, but then we picked up some negative signals. Epiphany kids were required to save half of their earnings in a bank account, but we found out he wasn't saving his money. He came up with excuses, but we knew something was up. He insisted he still had a job, but we had trouble verifying it. So we asked him for a meeting.

I started the discussion.

"Titus, you were doing so well here, but we have concerns about you, particularly your job and your money."

Unlike so many other kids I've worked with, he did not rant and rave, defending himself, and attacking us. He sat there calmly, almost stoic, always respectful.

"I'm doing some things I shouldn't be doing," he said.

"Such as?" Karen Hughes, our social worker, asked.

He shrugged.

"Come on, Titus," she continued. "Please be honest with us."

"I'm different out there," he said. "The Titus you see here is different from the one on the street."

We all knew what he was saying. He was dealing drugs back in his old neighborhood.

I felt terrible hearing this. We saw a nice young man with a pleasant personality who had a lot of potential. But I could imagine that out on a street corner in Queens he could be a totally different person, someone who was cool, calculating, and brutal. You had to have those qualities to make it as a drug dealer in New York City. You had to be able to kill and not think twice about it. We didn't know that Titus, but I'm sure he wasn't lying when he said that that Titus existed.

If a young man was to live at Epiphany, he had to make it in the world the right way. No one who dealt drugs for a living was going to stay at our place.

"Titus," I said, "of all the kids at Epiphany, I see you as the one with the best chance of making it." I told him we'd redouble our efforts at finding him another job, get him tutoring, and whatever else he needed to do things the right way. The other staff echoed these sentiments. But it was still up to Titus to decide.

"You know we can't let you stay here if you continue to deal drugs," I said. "So please take the next twenty-four hours to think it over. Let us know tomorrow what your decision is. I hope you take up our offer."

To my great relief, the next day Titus announced that he was giving up drug dealing and would cooperate with us in order to succeed legitimately. I was thrilled, and for the next two weeks everything seemed fine. But one night when I wasn't there Titus packed his bags and left. He gave no explanation to the counselors on duty. We never heard from him again.

When I came in to Epiphany the next morning and found out Titus had left, it was a sad moment. All of us really liked him. We could see the potential he had. I looked at him and could see, with his pleasant personality, leadership traits, and intelligence, a successful businessman or lawyer. We really believed he could make it. But somehow we weren't able to convince Titus that he could make it.

It is not being overly dramatic to state that we are in a war over the souls of our young. On one side are all the temptations—drugs, alcohol, quick money, peer pressure. We are on the other side. Our weapons in this war are compassion, respect, love, serving as a role model, steadfastness, courage, and faith in God. It is a constant battle. We win often, but not always.

Perseverance

I've learned from my work with young people that you can never predict which ones are going to accept your advice and guidance and follow a positive path, and which ones are not. So my philosophy has become to try my utmost with all. Put forth all the energy and effort necessary to reach out to adolescents, regardless of their exterior attitude. Anthony DeMello, S.J., when asked "What is love?" replied, "Take a look at a rose. Is it possible for the rose to say, 'I shall offer my fragrance to good people and withhold it from bad people'? Or can you imagine a lamp that withholds its rays from a wicked person who seeks to walk in its light? And observe how helplessly and indiscriminately a tree gives its shade to everyone; good and bad, young and old, high and low; to animals and humans and every living creature—even to the one who seeks to cut it down." That is exactly the inner disposition one must have in relation to young people.

One night I was searching through my files and happened upon a folder I long ago labeled "Letters from Kids." (I am a compulsive filer, always trying to create order out of the chaos of life.) It contained letters from young people I've counseled and worked with during the last twenty-two years. I had not looked at these letters in years, but they brought back a lot of good memories.

One letter that stood out was from a Carlton Jones. It is handwritten on United States Army stationary and dated 16

February '91. It is apparently in response to a letter I had written him.

Dear Mark,

I just received your letter. Thanks for thinking of me. It warmed my heart to know that I'm still thought of. You know, it gets lonely around here, so far away from home.

As for how I'm doing—I'm doing good. Tired and sore but feeling good. I have two weeks to go and I finish basic combat training and I get shipped off to Ft. Gordon, GA. I've marched distances as far as 6.2 miles (wow!) I'm in shape. Last week we had to qualify with our M-16 rifles and I qualified as expert. I got a medal pinned on me by the Lieutenant Colonel and everything.

Sometimes I lay down and think about my days at the Epiphany Youth Hostel. I know I was a pain, but that was the best place I've ever been. I will never forget y'all. Like I said before, I appreciate everything you've done for me. In a way you saved my life. You took me in and gave me a home, and I took advantage and became a responsible man. Married and with a career, thanks to all of you!

I hope we keep in contact with each other. If you ever need me for any reason, I'm here for you. Tell all the staff I miss them and I keep Epiphany in my prayers. Good luck to you and keep doing what y'all done for me. Tell the guys I said hi and write to me if they can. I'll keep writing.

Sincerely yours,

Carlton Jones

P.S. I saw the Super Bowl. Great game.

P.P.S. I'll know about the Persian Gulf sometime in April.

I am embarrassed to admit that I don't even remember Carlton Jones. I vaguely recollect writing to a young man who left Epiphany to join the Army, but if someone showed me a group photo of all the twenty young men who lived there in 1990–91, I doubt I would be able to pick him out. But that doesn't stop me from feeling great when reading his letter.

The next letter in the file was from a Hector Alvarez. Most of his letter is a complaint about loud music in the house and asking me to do something about it. But he closed it out with:

Mark, I would also like to thank you for all you have done for me. You have proved yourself time and time again not only as a director but as a friend. Thank you Mark because you know what? At times that's exactly what I needed; a friend!

He added, *"P.S. Have a nice day!"* and drew a little happy face.

Hector I do remember. Another Epiphany kid, he was about eighteen, homosexual, a big Madonna fan, and loved to dance around the house imitating her dancers. He was struck and killed by a car while trying to run across the Brooklyn-Queens Expressway. This happened about a year after I left Epiphany, and I never discovered the details. Yes, Hector I do remember.

Carlton and Hector. Two homeless teenagers who ended up at the same shelter, but with two drastically different results. Unfortunately, that is the reality of working with young people. You can never tell which ones are going to survive all the dangers and temptations of life, and which ones are not. A letter by Thomas Merton that I keep pinned to my bulletin board at work offers me the inspiration to keep going. It is entitled "Letter to a Young Activist" (*The Hidden Ground of Love: The*

Letters of Thomas Merton on Religious Experience and Social Concerns, William H. Shannon, ed., Harvest Books, 1993).

> Do not depend on the hope of results. When you are doing the sort of work you have taken on, essentially an apostolic work, you may have to face the fact that your work will be apparently worthless and achieve no result at all, if not perhaps results opposite to what you expect....Gradually you struggle less and less for an idea and more and more for specific people....In the end it is the reality of personal relationships that saves everything. The big results are not in your hands or mind, but they suddenly happen, and we can share in them; but there is no point in building our lives on this personal satisfaction, which may be denied to us and which after all is not that important.

"Gradually you struggle less and less for an idea and more and more for specific people." Yes, Fr. Merton was right. That is the spiritual journey—struggling less and less for ideas, and more and more for people, the people God brings into your life, be they family, neighbors, friends, coworkers, or the homeless man or woman or child you see on the street.

Leadership

Leaders will emerge among young people. It is difficult for adults to predict who those leaders will be. You may notice a teenager in a school or youth group with admirable qualities who you would like to see others follow and emulate. You can even encourage this, through direct appeal to this young person and through the messages you send the group. You can assign this person certain tasks that you hope will develop leadership qualities, or even assign a particular role that will do the same.

But my experience has taught me that it is in crisis when leaders emerge. This is true for the adult world, the most recent and obvious example being the World Trade Center tragedy, when certain individuals stood out for their bravery and leadership throughout a frightening time. It is no different with young people. In fearful times, in times of crisis, some among them will stand out, and it may not be the class president, team captain, or an officer in the Catholic Youth Organization. It may very well be someone you would not have chosen. But that doesn't matter. What matters is the adult's willingness, ability, and skill to work with that young person who is a leader among his or her peers.

In 1992 I became director of St. Christopher's, a residential treatment center (RTC) for troubled youth located in Dobbs Ferry, a small town in Westchester County, New York. Seventy-two teenage boys and girls lived there. Most of these young people were originally from very poor and dangerous neighborhoods of New York City. Some came to St. Christopher's directly from their homes. These kids were often involved in criminal activity such as drug dealing, using drugs, gang membership, and petty larceny. Their parents often begged a Family Court judge to have their children removed from home and placed in an RTC.

Other teenagers came to St. Christopher's from foster homes. These kids often had no parents, or parents who were in jail, sick with AIDS, or so deeply involved in drugs that they were incapable of raising a family. But many young people do not do well living with foster parents. An RTC is the next step for them.

Some young people arrived at an RTC directly from a psychiatric hospital. These kids had usually been hospitalized for suicidal gestures or severe depression or psychosis. When doctors at a psych hospital believe such a young person is ready to work his or her way back into the mainstream of society, placement in an RTC is often the first step.

St. Christopher's was situated on the banks of the Hudson River, directly across from the majestic Palisade cliffs. It was an absolutely stunning location. Unfortunately, the RTC itself was in poor condition. The teenagers lived in cottages that were roach infested and covered with graffiti. Windows were broken or missing. Doors hung off hinges. Furniture was dilapidated. Two plastic milk crates tied to a fence served as basketball hoops. A baseball diamond was overrun with weeds. The place was completely depressing.

My predecessor had been there for twelve years. I met him once, before I actually took over. A man in his late fifties, he seemed very nice and greeted me with a smile. He treated me with respect as he showed me the director's house that had been his but would now be mine. But he did look worn, tired. I was told that at some point several years earlier he became overwhelmed by all the problems and simply stopped trying to hold the place together. The RTC spiraled downward. Without strong leadership at the top, staff became complacent and the kids took advantage. I was told that full-scale riots were not uncommon, with twenty, thirty, or even all seventy-two of them out during the middle of the night destroying property and assaulting staff. The police were practically fixtures on campus. The director was finally fired when kids began to leave the grounds to commit crimes in the surrounding community. I was shown press clippings that detailed auto theft, burglary, indecent exposure on the main avenue in town, and assaults on citizens. Dobbs Ferry was an upper-middle-class section of Westchester County that was unaccustomed to such things. A "Let's Close St. Christopher's" movement took root and was actively lobbying local and state representatives to do just that.

So Luis Medina, the executive director of St. Christopher's, advertised the position, I saw it in the *New York Times,* interviewed, and was hired. When my first day of employment arrived, I was nervous but also determined to succeed. I spent most of that day introducing myself to the staff and teenagers. I asked each staff member how long he or she had worked there. Most reported they had been there ten years or longer. I also asked, "In your time here, how does the program now rate in terms of quality?" Without exception the answer was, "This is the worst I have seen it." There was no other way around it—I was inheriting a mess. I spent the next few days familiarizing myself with the program and trying to get a handle on what my main challenges would be. Nothing terrible occurred other than a few one-on-one fistfights that staff members quickly broke up.

At the end of my fourth day I was preparing to leave for home at about 6:00 P.M. My predecessor had not yet moved out of the house, so I commuted to my home in Brooklyn about an hour away. As I walked to my car a staff member approached and handed me a photocopied handwritten note:

Rally Tonight
Behind the School
7:00 P.M.
To Protest the Rodney King Verdict
All Residents— Be There!!

I had not heard the news, but the officers accused of beating Rodney King had been acquitted of assault earlier that day. South-central Los Angeles was in flames. Riots had broken out in other cities. And here I was in an almost exclusively white section of Westchester, with seventy-one adolescents who were African American or Hispanic. Only one was white. The setting for a disaster was staged.

One of our social workers figured out which young man was behind the rally. His name was Jamel, and he had been at the RTC for several years. The social worker told me Jamel was one of those kids who could be positive at times while destructive at others. She said he had severe emotional difficulties; he had tried to hang himself from a tree a few months earlier, only to be rescued by the staff. But, I was told, Jamel could be reasoned with and did have a large influence over the rest of the population.

Based on what I just learned about him, I certainly would not have selected Jamel to lead his peers during this difficult time. But who I would have selected really didn't matter right now. What mattered was that this was the young man the kids looked up to and listened to, and I had to deal with that fact and deal with him.

I wrestled with the notion of trying to convince Jamel to outright cancel the rally. I knew it would be fruitless to demand that it be cancelled. It was obvious to me that the teenagers were in control of St. Christopher's and had been for several years. They did what they wanted to—went to school when they felt like it, smoked pot when they wanted to, and went into town to commit crimes when the mood struck. I knew that at this time the adults ostensibly in charge of the program did not have the power to stop something the youth were determined to do.

I asked where I could find Jamel. Told he was probably in his cottage, I went there and asked the staff on duty if he was around. They told me he was, and I found him in the cottage recreation room. I introduced myself and asked if we could talk. He agreed. Jamel was sixteen, stocky build, a light-skinned African American. His mood was calm, pensive. He listened without flying off the handle. He acknowledged right away that he was the one behind the rally, had made the posters, photocopied, and distributed them. I quickly judged that he was intent on having this rally, but I also had the sense that what the social worker told me was correct—he could be reasoned with. So I offered Jamel a compromise: Have the rally, but move it indoors to the campus chapel. I made the case that an outdoor rally could get out of hand quickly, would be hard to control, and would be too loud for the neighbors next door. Jamel agreed to this, and I silently breathed a sigh of relief.

When 7:00 P.M. came I entered the chapel on grounds. All seventy-two teenagers were there as well as most of the staff. Except for one female teenager and a psychologist, I was the sole white person there. It made me remember one of the questions I was asked during my interview weeks earlier: "How will you deal with the fact that you are replacing an African American man who was here for twelve years, virtually all the teenagers are minority, and so are most of the staff?" This was not a new question for me. In fact, I have been asked some variation of it at every step in my career, and I always give the same response: "I am here to help kids who are in need. I don't care what race they are, religion, or sexual orientation. I will be sensitive to cultural factors. I realize many of these young people have not had positive experiences with white people, and I will have to work hard to convince them that I am here to help them build a better life. But I've done it before and I believe I can do it again."

A big-screen television was on at the front of the chapel. It showed L.A. in flames, people rioting and looting. President Bush then appeared at a news conference to proclaim, "The jury has spoken. This is the American way of justice, trial by a jury of one's peers."

"Nice going, George, nice going," I thought. "Thanks for helping me out here."

Someone turned the television off and Jamel took the floor. The residents and staff were seated in a large circle. Jamel stood in the middle and began.

"When I heard that these policemen were found not guilty, after what they had done to Rodney King, I was furious. I'm half-black, so I feel like he's my brother in some way. My first reaction was that we should do in this town what they are doing now in L.A. We should burn the town down. But then I thought some more about it. And I realized that this is not the answer. That won't do any good. The answer is to follow the example of Dr. Martin Luther King Jr. We need to organize ourselves and work for change and fight racism, but in a nonviolent way. That's what we need to do, and that's what I'm going to do with my life."

Everybody clapped, and I went "Phew."

Then another young man stood up. Jorge was Hispanic, maybe fourteen or fifteen years old. He was short, thin, a wisp of a kid. Even though I had only been there four days, I knew he was one of the negative ringleaders on grounds. Tears streamed down his face as he spoke.

"When are we going to wake up? When are we going to do something about the racism in our world? How about the racism here in this program? This place is racist. The kids here kiss the butt of the white people."

He pointed to the psychologist sitting near him.

"They kiss her ass."

He then pointed to me.

"Now they'll start kissing his."

"I think we should riot," he continued. "I think we should go into town and burn it down. In fact, that's what I'm going to do right now. Who's going with me?"

He marched toward the chapel door. I held my breath, wondering how many kids would go with him. I knew it was not an impossibility for some or all of them to do so.

Thankfully, not one kid left with him. A staff member followed him out of the chapel to calm him down. Other staff in the chapel then began to stand up to speak. All of them were African Americans, some of them old enough to be veterans of the 1960's civil rights movement. They talked about marching with Dr. King, Ralph Abernathy, and Jesse Jackson, and they said things the kids needed to hear. They spoke of how it was right to be outraged over the Rodney King verdict, but the way to fight racism was through education, organization, and political power. They had witnessed violence, and it was not the way to accomplish a greater good.

When it seemed like all had been said, Jamel rose in order to wrap things up. I raised my hand and asked if I could say something. All eyes turned and there was a long silence. Again, this was only my fourth day there; I knew a few of the staff and hardly any of the kids. It was a racially charged moment for the entire country, not just our residence. By now the psychologist had left, so I was the only white staff member in a crowd of almost one hundred.

I introduced myself. "My name is Mark Redmond. I'm the new director here. I've met a few of you, and I'm looking forward to knowing all of you soon.

"First of all, I want to say that I agree with everything the staff has said here tonight. They have given all of us good advice. Second, I want you to know that I think what happened in that courtroom today was a terrible injustice. Rodney King was beaten, everyone who has seen that videotape can see that, and I can't understand how the jurors let those policemen off.

"But you know what? Injustices have been happening for years. There were terrible injustices that took place in the 1980s. There were miscarriages of justice in the '70s. There were terrible injustices in the '60s. Look what happened to Dr. King then. But there were injustices before that, in the '50s, in the '40s, and before that. The fact is that there have been great injustices in every society and in every age since time began. And there will be more in the years to come. They're bound to happen. It may not be an injustice against an African American. It might be an injustice against a white person, or an Hispanic, or an Asian. But there will always be injustices.

"The question for each of you kids is: Where will you be when the next injustice occurs? What position will you be in to do something about it when it happens? That's what you have to think about. Before coming to work here I ran a shelter for homeless teenagers in Brooklyn. We had a young man there, he was white and he was a heavy metal punker. He dressed in all leather, he had about five earrings, a nose ring, big black boots, and a spiked Mohawk haircut. He had been living in an abandoned building as a squatter when he was kicked out and then came to us. He kept talking about the need to change the world, to create better opportunities for the homeless, and to fight the oppression, poverty, and racism that envelop society. Know what I told him? I told him I agreed with everything he wanted to do, but I wanted to know how he was going to do it when he was homeless, uneducated, and penniless. I told him that he had to clean up his act first, get an education, and situate himself so he could really do something about poverty and racism, because no one was listening to him as he yelled up from the sidewalk.

"He didn't want to hear that, but I'm asking you to hear that. The best response to the Rodney King verdict takes place in school tomorrow. If you're really concerned, you're going to go in there and educate yourself, and do it the next day, and the next day. Look at Malcolm X. He was a drug dealer, a pimp, a loser. What did he do when he was put in jail? He studied his butt off! He taught himself to read, he educated himself, and he ended up being an important leader. That should be your goal, and it starts tomorrow for each and every one of you."

I sat down. There was silence, and I wondered how my speech had been received. Then the clapping began. Kids, staff, everyone. I felt great.

Jamel then stood up.

"Will everyone please rise?" he asked. They did.

"Please join hands." Some of the kids were reluctant, but everyone complied.

Then Jamel began: "Our Father, who art in heaven..."

It was a wonderful moment, certainly for me and I believe for everyone there, as we said the Lord's Prayer, giving thanks to God for all that had transpired that evening and asking his guidance throughout the tumultuous days that were to follow in our country.

When we finished praying I went up to Jamel and shook his hand, thanking him for what he said and did. Everyone exited the chapel peacefully and went to their cottages without incident.

The next day word spread among the day staff that I had prevented a race riot.

"It wasn't me," I protested, "Jamel really did it."

"Take the credit, Mark," advised one colleague, "because they'll soon be blaming you for bad stuff that wasn't your fault. Enjoy this moment while it lasts." That proved to be true.

In this type of work, it is virtually impossible to keep track of every youth after leaving your program. Unless a young person comes back to visit or calls, I rarely know how he or she has fared in life after leaving us. I can't tell you how the kids who were in the chapel that day did in the world beyond St. Christopher's. I do know that Jamel signed himself out of our program a few weeks after the rally and ended up living on the streets of Brooklyn. When I found out he was homeless, I helped him get into the shelter I had previously run, Epiphany, but he eventually left there too. That was the last I heard of or about him, and I can only hope and pray things went well for him. I will always be grateful to him for what he did and said that evening. As Dr. Martin Luther King once wrote, "The ultimate measure of a man is not where he stands in moments of comfort and convenience, but where he stands at times of challenge and controversy." That April 1992 evening was such a time, and Jamel came through as a man of character, a true leader.

Courage

There are times when it takes absolute courage to face a situation with a young person. A crisis erupts out of nowhere, and you have to respond. Every second counts and you are not afforded the luxury of mulling over alternative courses of action. Times like these are when you mutter a quick prayer to God for guidance and strength, and then you plunge ahead, counting on his assistance.

I was required to live on grounds of St. Christopher's. I commuted to my home in Brooklyn for the first few weeks of work, but then I moved into the house right next to the campus reserved for the person in my position. There were two phones in that house; one was a phone just as you'd have in any ordinary house in America, the other was a direct line from the campus. That phone was specifically for emergencies.

I was only living in this house for two days when the work phone rang shortly after 9:00 P.M. I immediately recognized the voice of Bob Hinton, the evening administrator on duty.

"Mark, you'd better get over here."

"What's the problem, Bob?"

"Remember that kid Michael Robinson, the kid who ran away from here a few weeks ago? Well he's back, and the kids say he has a gun."

A kid with a gun is the number one fear of anyone who works with troubled teenagers. When I first arrived at St.

Christopher's, there were many young people there who carried weapons. We confiscated knives, Ninja sticks, brass knuckles. I had a file cabinet drawer filled with them. But a gun was something entirely different. None of us in this line of work mention guns, but it's always in the back of our minds. It's almost as if to talk about it makes the chances of some kid having one greater. So we carry on in our jobs, counseling kids, giving them guidance, helping them with school, hoping that none of them will ever try to sneak one in.

Michael Robinson. I had had a run-in with him my third day on the job. Age fifteen, he had a nasty habit of sexually intimidating younger, smaller boys in his cottage by waking them up in the middle of the night and waving his penis in their face. When I learned of this, I warned him we would notify the police and press charges if he did it again. He stopped, but a few days later he hopped the fence and left our place on his own. His social worker called his family to see if he was there, but they hadn't seen him.

But now Bob was telling me he was back, supposedly with a gun. I asked him exactly where on our property Michael was standing.

"We last saw him up by the entrance, standing on the driveway. The kids say he's here to shoot his girlfriend's new boyfriend."

St. Christopher's was co-ed, and boys and girls were always pairing off, breaking up, and starting a romance with somebody else. When he lived at our place Michael had a girlfriend on grounds. When he left she hooked up with another young man. Someone called Michael and told him this, and he was now apparently back here to kill him.

"Bob, I'm going to call the police and then I'm coming right over." When I started at St. Christopher's I was told that our relationship with the local police was not a good one. The program had been out of control for so long and the police had frequently been called in to quell riots and break up drug parties. One cop told me, "We've been to your place so often we feel like we should set up a precinct there." Luis Medina, the executive director of St. Christopher's, told me when I started, "Your goal is to see if you can keep us out of the police blotter in the local paper for two weeks in a row."

But this time there was no avoiding calling the police. I dialed 911, and when the desk sergeant answered I told him our situation. Since I believed that Michael was standing near our entrance, I asked the sergeant to tell whomever he sent to refrain from turning on their siren. I believed that Michael would hear this and run away before the police could apprehend him.

"Don't tell us how to do our job," was his response. He hung up before I could give my rationale for the request.

I left my house and ran over to the administrative office where I knew Bob would be.

"Bob, are you absolutely sure he's got a gun?"

"He went up to a girl who was walking to the infirmary and showed it to her, telling her he's here to blow away this other boy. The girl freaked out and ran into her cottage and told her staff. She's really shook up. The staff think she's telling the truth about the gun."

Bob and I left his office and started crossing the eighteen acres of our campus. In a few minutes, about seventy yards away, I spotted Michael Robinson. He paced up and down the top of our driveway, where it met the street. It was dark out, but we had some fairly powerful lights there, so we could see it was definitely him. I stopped advancing, as did Bob. I could tell Michael didn't see us. I knew I wasn't going to approach him to try something stupid like taking the gun off him. I did wonder what Michael's next move would be. Would he head over to the cottage where he knew his ex-girlfriend's boyfriend lived?

Would he go to her cottage instead? And why was he just pacing near the entrance to our facility? What was he waiting for? Above all, I prayed for the police to arrive.

About thirty seconds later I spotted a police car coming down the street and approaching our driveway. Despite his statement to me on the phone, the sergeant had apparently passed my advice along. There was no siren. Michael did not hear them approaching. When I saw that car coming, I rushed toward the scene. I knew anything could happen. Michael could spot the car and start blasting away at it. Or the cops could see him with the gun and start shooting at him. This had the potential of violence and tragedy, and I was scared.

Thank God neither possibility occurred. The police drove down the driveway and practically ran Michael over. I was now about twenty-five yards away and could see the look of shock on his face when he realized it was a police car. Rather than shooting, he immediately started sprinting away. He headed across our lawn, over the fence, and onto the street.

At that point two more police cars coming onto the scene pursued him. Within five minutes the cars returned and Michael was in the back seat of one. They led him out, in handcuffs, and they brought him over to some bushes on the perimeter of our grounds. I watched him point to a spot, and the police started searching. Apparently he had tossed the gun while making his exit, and the police had convinced him to show them where it was. They found the gun, drove him away, and that was the last we ever saw him. I later learned he was sent to a youth detention facility.

First the Rodney King experience and now this. I was starting to understand just how challenging St. Christopher's was going to be. There was not going to be any quick fix. There rarely is when it comes to dealing with young people. Patience, wisdom, compassion, and prayer are required more than anything else.

Setting Limits

It is important for adults to set the standards for young people in terms of acceptable and unacceptable behavior. This is what they need, and it is what they want. It is important to remember that. Teenagers may not act like it, but they are silently waiting and hoping for you to set and maintain the boundaries of behavior. Adolescents know that they are unable to be independent, to take complete charge of their life. They are not psychologically or materially ready to do this, and know it. They need adults to put brakes on their behavior. It is your job to do this.

You can count on teenagers testing those boundaries. They may even complain bitterly. Do not be fooled. Do not give in. They want those limits to be set and held, and it is important for you to do so.

I was only at St. Christopher's about two months when one night I left my house shortly after 11:00 to do a quick tour of the grounds. It was early summer and warm outside. I stopped in at the administrative office to chat with the administrator on duty for that night, Saul Berger. Mr. Berger had been working at St. Christopher's for over a year.

"How are things on the campus tonight?" I asked him.

"The Hayden Cottage girls are a little restless. They're mad at their staff about something."

I was surprised to hear this. There were seven cottages on grounds, and the girls in Hayden Cottage gave us the fewest problems. There were twelve girls in Hayden, and they always went to school on time, did their chores, kept the house clean, no fighting. I sat in on a house meeting there two weeks earlier, and the staff was completely in control. In fact, I remember thinking they were too in control. The staff reprimanded individual girls for things they had done wrong, and the girls remained mute. I picked up an oppressive feeling in the cottage, but I decided to put it on the back burner. Most house meetings I had been to at St. Christopher's were just the opposite; staff were begging kids to do chores, keep the house clean, wake up on time, with the kids responding by cursing out the staff. If I had to choose between a little oppression and a lot of mayhem, I'd choose the former, for now anyway. I realized staff in Hayden needed to ease up and focus on building relationships with the girls, but in the midst of everything else occurring on the campus, it wasn't my biggest immediate concern.

I asked Mr. Berger to walk the grounds with me. We left the chapel and were about halfway across the property when we spotted the Hayden girls exiting from their cottage.

"What are they doing?" I asked him.

"Oh crap," he replied. "I hope this isn't the start of a riot."

Riot. I had heard the word used many times in my nine weeks on the job. The campus had a history of riots, with gangs of kids beating each other, destroying property, and assaulting staff. I was told riots could go on for hours and often required police intervention. I was told there had been a very bad one about two months before I arrived, during the day at the school on our grounds. The police had been called in, several kids were arrested, and one school aide was still out on disability with an injury.

"There's nothing worse than a late night riot," Mr. Berger continued. "We're down to only one staff member per cottage, and the kids know that. I'd better call the other cottages and tell the counselors to block the doors. If the Hayden girls get all the other kids to come out, we're in big trouble."

Berger ran back to the chapel to make his phone calls. I stood there watching the Hayden girls walking together as a pack in the pitch dark. My heart was absolutely pounding. How do I get this under control? How do I get them back in? What if all seventy-two kids come out to join them? Eleven years of working with troubled youth had not prepared me for this.

There were four or five counselors still on duty who were supposed to leave at 11:00 P.M. but had remained to complete paperwork. They came over to me, and we watched the girls exit out our driveway, start to head into town, but then return to campus almost immediately.

"They're scared to go into town," said Mona Warren, an African American woman who I already knew was one of our best counselors.

"Boys would have gone," she continued, "and they would have done some damage in town. We're lucky."

Saul Berger returned. "I called all the cottages and told the staff to stand in the doorways and not let anyone out. I don't know if it'll work. Twelve kids can easily overrun one counselor. Let's keep our fingers crossed."

The six of us huddled up. "How do we stop this?" I asked. "How do we get those girls back in? What have you done in the past?"

"We take them to McDonald's," replied one of the staff.

"You what?" I responded.

"Yeah, we've done that before and it works. You tell them that if they agree to get into one of the vans we'll take them to McDonald's. We buy them some Big Macs and when they get back they're tired out and usually go right into the cottage."

"So you reward them for rioting?" I asked.

He just stared at the ground.

"Well we're not doing that anymore," I said. "Anyone else have a suggestion?"

"These girls are following one or two leaders," said Mona. "We've got to physically restrain those leaders and forcibly drag them into the cottage. Once they are in, the others will be frightened and come in on their own."

"Who are the leaders in that cottage?" I asked.

"Maryanne and Charlotte," said one person.

"No, no, it's Charlotte and Wendy," said someone else.

"No, both of you are wrong, they're all following Jessica," came yet another opinion.

"I'm against physically restraining any of them," said Mr. Berger. "You put one of those girls down on the ground, out here in the open, and I guarantee you that kids are going to come pouring out of those buildings and start wailing away on us."

Silence. We all stood in that huddle, everyone looking at me for answers. I was their new leader, and I didn't have a clue what to do.

But I had to come up with something.

"No physical restraining," I said. "Let's follow them, try to get them to talk to us, and see if we can convince them to go back in peacefully."

By now the girls were at the opposite end of the campus, standing in front of a boy's cottage, screaming up at them, trying to get them to come out and join them. Some girls picked up rocks and threw them at windows. A male counselor stood in the doorway, arms folded across his chest. Mr. Berger's plan was working. The boys weren't leaving. They were hanging out their bedroom windows, hooting and hollering, daring the girls to bare their breasts, but at least they weren't joining them.

As we approached the girls they ran from us. They headed for another cottage, this time a female one, and again threw rocks and screamed at the top of their lungs. Again no one joined them, but the screaming and yelling emanating from our property must have been heard by every household in the neighborhood. And it was now past midnight. Berger left us to go back to the administrator's office for a few minutes. When he returned he said, "The phone is ringing off the hook. The neighbors are furious. I'm sure we'll be hearing from the police soon."

As we approached the girls they again ran and proceeded to the next cottage. And the next. And the next. We continued to run after them. At one point I circled after them as they ran through the backyard of a boys' cottage, and a bar of soap thrown from a bedroom window whizzed by my head, barely missing me. I looked up and saw heads ducking from the window, but it was too dark to recognize anyone. "Man," I said to myself, "this is dangerous."

By 1:00 A.M. we were back at the boys cottage where they had started. The boys were still up, and everyone was still screaming and breaking windows. We were now on our second lap of the campus.

And then the girls headed back toward their own cottage. I watched them go inside. I couldn't believe it. Finally. Mr. Berger, Mona Warren, and the rest of us followed them in. When I entered someone handed me a phone. "It's the police. They want to speak to someone in charge."

I spoke into the receiver. "Yes, officer."

"You guys okay over there? We've received a ton of calls from your neighbors. Do you want assistance?"

Remembering the directive to refrain from involving the police unless absolutely necessary, I declined the offer.

"No thanks, officer, I think we've got it under control now."

The girls were assembled in the cottage rec room. Despite the late hour and that they had been running for several hours, they were still extremely agitated and vocal. It was just a chorus of shouting and yelling in that room. Mona tried to gain control. No success. So did Saul Berger. Then I pounded my hand on a table and yelled as loud as I could, "Girls! Girls! What is this all about? What is the problem? Why are you doing this?"

Maybe there was a split second of silence. Maybe. But I couldn't get them under control either. It was impossible to decipher what they were upset about and why they were rioting.

Finally a fifteen-year-old African American named Helen jumped up on a coffee table and started complaining about their cottage manager, Mrs. Bartley.

"She took our money! She took our allowance money and bought a coffee pot for the cottage! None of us even drink coffee! Only she and the staff drink coffee. We didn't get our allowance money, and when she gets back from vacation we're going to kick her ass!"

"Yeah, yeah," the other girls screamed. "We're going to kick Mrs. Bartley's ass!"

I stood there, incredulous. That's what this was all about—allowance money and a coffee pot? I couldn't believe it. Mrs. Bartley was a kindly old woman, African American, who had spent her entire career in youth work. She was presently on a two-week vacation, far away from this madness.

I slammed my fist on the table again. "I'll straighten out your allowance money tomorrow. I'll look into this coffee pot business too. But you've got to promise me you're not going to run around the grounds like this any more because..."

"No you won't!" It was Helen, this time right in my face. "You're a liar. You're going to take her side. You never listen to us."

"Never listen to you?" I thought. "Take Mrs. Bartley's side? I've been here a couple of weeks, how can you say that about me?" But that would be using logic, and at this point these girls were not into logic. So I tried a different strategy.

"Girls, if you are a parent and you have seven children, six of whom are being really bad and one of whom is behaving well, don't you think it's natural that the good one is not going to get the same attention as the bad ones? That is what has been happening. The other cottages have been behaving so badly and you've been so good that I haven't had the chance to pay much attention to what is going on here. But now I will because..."

They drowned me out. My little analogy was not hitting home. Mona once again tried to take over, directing girls into the shower. I backed into a corner of the rec room, feeling overwhelmed. Miraculously, after a few minutes it appeared that Mona was gaining momentum. Some were listening to her, heading toward the bathroom. It was still mayhem, but in my mind the tide was turning in our favor.

I exited from the front door of the cottage. I looked at my watch—2:00 A.M. I scanned the campus. Lights were still on in bedrooms, so kids in the other cottages were still up and probably pretty wired. What a night, what a frigging night, but at least the worst was over.

A counselor came out of Hayden and ran over to me. "The girls are out again, Mark."

"No they're not," I insisted. "I was just in there. I saw Mona getting them into the showers."

"Maybe one or two, but most of them jumped out the bedroom windows and are running around again."

I turned and spotted the silhouette of a gang of girls on the run, heading for another cottage.

Unbelievable. Unreal.

I grabbed the counselor by the shoulders. "Go in there and tell Mona Warren to come out. Tell Mr. Berger I want him too, and anyone else. Leave one counselor in there with the girls. Anyone else, I want them here with me."

In less than a minute I had the original team of six with whom I had huddled three hours earlier. We huddled again.

"We're going to full physical restraint, people," I said. "You two are a team, you two, and Berger and I are a team. We will systematically restrain one girl at a time and drag her into Hayden. Try to do it whenever they run near the cottage. Try not to drag a girl all the way across grounds. It's better if you do it when they are close by." I was still cognizant of the fact that other kids were up and could easily join the fray if they felt one of their own was being abused.

We broke into our teams. Berger and I hid behind a tree near Hayden, and when a group of girls ran by we'd jump out, come up behind one, lift her by the elbows and carry her inside. The other twosomes did the same. Eventually Mona stationed herself by the door to receive a girl as we brought her up. Mona would take her from us and lead her down the hallway and right into the shower.

Within half an hour ten of the twelve were inside. I was physically and emotionally exhausted. I just couldn't wait for the night to end. One of the counselors approached me.

"Lily and Wendy are still out. They're over by the side of the cottage."

In retrospect I wish I had just said, "Screw it. Let them come in on their own." But I was thinking about what had happened earlier on, when I thought we had everyone in, and then they all left. This time I wanted everyone in.

"Let's get Lily first," I said.

Four of us approached her. Lily was new to the program, even newer than I was. She had arrived about a week earlier, and I knew nothing about her. She was a tall Hispanic girl, about age fourteen. I had yet to read her psychological and psychiatric profiles.

"Come on, Lily, let's go inside," said a female counselor.

Lily turned her back on us and walked away from the cottage.

"Lily, I mean it. It's over for the night. Everyone's going in," repeated the counselor. But Lily kept walking.

"Let's grab her," I told the male staff member with me. We tried what is termed "touch control," putting our arms around her shoulders to accompany her in the direction we wished. But she shrugged her shoulders violently and broke free. She started to run.

"Let's take her down," I told him. We ran after her, and I grabbed her upper body as he took her legs. We forced her to the ground, with the intention of carrying her into the cottage.

Lily screamed at the top of her lungs. "My knee! My knee! Oh my God, you bastards, my knee!" With that, a group of four boys watching from a nearby cottage ran out and pounced on top of us. One of them was Kevin, a big tall fifteen year old. I later found out that Lily was his girlfriend and he felt obliged to protect her. (A girlfriend after she'd only been there a week? I would learn that is how quickly males and females hooked up at our program.) Other male staff saw us being attacked and jumped on top of them. I was now on the bottom of a rumble, scared out of my mind because I knew there was a good chance at least one of those boys had a knife and would not hesitate to use it.

We rolled around on the ground, Lily still screaming in pain, clutching her knee. The males managed to stand up, clutching at each other, men wrapping their arms around teenage boys, who fought back. I played rugby in college, and it felt like I was in the middle of a scrum again—a meandering thicket of arms, legs, and torsos. We landed on the hood of a parked car, rolled across the hood and onto the ground. Finally one staff member grabbed Kevin by the collar, and screamed into his face. "Stop it, Kevin, stop! Someone is going to get hurt! Stop!" Slowly, slowly, I watched the veil of reason cross Kevin's face. He began to loosen his grip on the counselor. The counselor did the same. One by one arms stopped clutching, and we untangled ourselves, our scrum falling apart to reveal sweaty, dirty bodies strewn across the ground.

The boys backed away, retreating to their cottage. By now several counselors surrounded Lily, who still lay on the ground, sobbing. I approached her, and she pulled a clump of grass out of the ground and threw it at me.

"I hate you, you white son of a bitch," she screamed.

I said nothing.

"We should get her to a hospital," someone said.

A counselor drove a van over. Staff lifted her in as she wailed in pain, and they drove her to the hospital. (She was X-rayed and seen by a doctor. His diagnosis was that there was absolutely nothing wrong, she was faking the injury. I know he was correct because I watched her walking around without so much as a limp the next day.)

That still left Wendy to bring inside. I had figured out by now that Wendy was indeed one of the leaders of the cottage and one of the strategists of the night's revolt. She was fourteen, Hispanic, and built like a fireplug. A burn mark ran across the left side of her face, from forehead to chin. She had a nasty mouth and a disposition to match. She stood a few yards out-side of Hayden, defying us to force her in. She eyed me, and I eyed her back. I turned to the male staff member who had assisted me with Lily.

"Leave her," I said. "She can go in on her own when she wants to."

I had had enough physical activity for one night.

I went home and collapsed into bed. I looked at the clock on my nightstand. It was a few minutes past 3:00 A.M.

I was scheduled to chair a meeting of all campus administrators at 9:00 that morning. I woke up at 8:30 and called the administrator on duty to reschedule the meeting for 11:00. After only five-plus hours of sleep, I was still exhausted. I was also discouraged. I lay in bed wondering if I had bitten off more than I could chew when I accepted this job. I knew it was going to be a challenge, but not like this. It was just all too much— the problems, the ineffective staff, the violence of the kids. I thought about the boys who had attacked us a few hours earlier; would they try it again today? I thought about the bar of soap missing my head by millimeters, and Lily throwing dirt at me as she cursed me out. Did all the kids feel this way? As I lay in bed thinking about all this and feeling despondent, I heard the voice of a cottage supervisor outside below my window. "I heard they had a riot out here last night," she told someone. "They ran our new director around until 3:00 in the morning."

At 10:45 I dragged myself out of the house and onto the campus. I walked toward the conference room where the administrator's meeting would be held. On the way there, Kevin, of all people, approached me. I stopped in my tracks, wondering if he was going to threaten or even strike me. Instead, he held out his hand.

"I'm sorry for what I did last night. I just lost my head when I saw my girlfriend hurt like that. Please forgive me."

I was dumbfounded. "Yes. I forgive you, Kevin. But don't ever interfere with a staff member again who is restraining a resident, I don't care if it's your girlfriend or not."

I shook his hand and continued toward the meeting. Then one of the girls from Hayden walked over to me. It was one of the girls I had lifted by the elbows into the cottage only hours before.

"Mr. Redmond, we're still going on the beach trip today, right? You're not mad at us or anything for last night, are you?"

She grinned as she said this. And then I realized that she meant it. She really expected me to just shrug off what had happened and let them go on a lovely summer outing. I just shook my head and kept walking, not even bothering to answer her.

I entered the conference room. No one had yet arrived. I sat at the head of the table, still pondering the events of the previous night. In the doorway appeared Linda Rodgers. Linda was an African American woman in her late twenties. She was the manager of one of the boys' cottages, and someone who I believed to be competent. She saw me and said, "Mark, we are behind you on this one hundred percent. Speaking for all the supervisors, we are going to support you in whatever you want to do. What those girls did last night has happened many times here, and it's time to teach them and every other kid here that once and for all, this kind of behavior is unacceptable." For the first time in twelve hours I felt uplifted. The other supervisors showed up within the next few minutes, and they reiterated Linda's message—Mark, we're with you, let's all work together so this never happens again.

We sat around the conference table and strategized. We quickly reached consensus on one point: The Hayden girls had to be hit with some serious consequences. If all the other kids saw that, they'd know the days of "off to McDonald's we go" were over. That meant, for starters, no beach trip for Hayden.

"Who is organizing the trip?" I asked.

A supervisor raised her hand.

"Can you get all the other cottages out of here and to the beach within the next two hours?" I asked.

She said she would.

Mona Warren was at the meeting.

"We've got to isolate the leaders of Hayden from the rest of the followers in there," she stated.

I thought it made sense, and so did the others.

"Can we send Wendy to our other campus, even if only for a few days?" she asked.

St. Christopher's ran another RTC, only for females, about a half hour away. I picked up the phone and called the assistant director there. She agreed to take Wendy on an interim basis.

"How about Lily and Helen?" asked Linda. "They are leaders in Hayden too. Where can we put them?"

"How about the cottage that's empty and being renovated?" someone asked. We were in the middle of a campus-wide renovation program, and there was one cottage that was not being used.

"If you throw three beds in there, I'll take those girls and stay overnight with them," offered Barbara Cook, a cottage supervisor.

"I'll join you," said Linda.

We had our plan in place. We took a break, and I toured the campus. I watched kids from the other cottages enter our vans and head for the beach. Two Hayden girls walked over toward me.

"When are the vans coming for us?" they asked.

I just shook my head. I still could not believe that these girls viewed their behavior as nothing out of the ordinary and that they should still get rewarded the next day.

By 1:00 P.M. every cottage was empty except for Hayden. I asked if Norm Ashley, one of our recreation workers, was still around. He was. Norm had muscles upon muscles, and I wanted him around to help us send Wendy off.

"Please ask him to come over," I said, "and tell Wendy's social worker to bring the car over here, with the engine running." We then called for Wendy.

She strutted into the office, a look of absolute defiance across her face. She plopped her body into a chair, arms folded across her chest.

"What the hell do you people want?" she said.

"We're taking you for a little ride," I answered.

"The hell you are!" she responded and bolted from her chair in an attempt to escape. Norm and a few others grabbed her and took her to the car outside. She screamed and fought. They got her up to the open car door but couldn't get her inside. I looked and saw that she had wedged her foot under the rear tire. I reached under and used both of my hands to pry her foot loose. With that, she and two counselors tumbled into the back seat, someone else shut the door, and I slapped the trunk, yelling to the social worker, "Go!" She put the pedal to the metal, the tires squealed, and she sped out of there.

Now for Lily and Helen, Linda volunteered to bring them to the vacant cottage. The other supervisors and I went on ahead. A few minutes later Linda arrived with the two girls. We assembled in the rec room.

"Girls, you are staying here," I said.

They immediately started wailing, but Linda and Barbara quickly calmed them down, and we left.

So now we were on to our final destination of the day—Hayden Cottage. Mona, five other supervisors, and I entered. We asked the counselor on duty to assemble the girls in the rec room. As they came in, I could see they were frightened. Their demeanor was quite different from what I had witnessed only hours before in that very room. I could hear them whispering to each other, "Where's Wendy? Why isn't Lily here? How about Helen, where's Helen?" They were without their leaders, and they knew it.

I spoke to them.

"Ladies, what you did last night was outrageous. Absolutely outrageous. Destroying property, trying to get all the other kids up out of bed, disrupting our neighbors—none of this will ever be tolerated again."

Mona took it from there.

"You are on total house restriction. No one is allowed outside for any reason whatsoever. You will wake up at 8:00 each morning and clean this house all day long. You will break only for breakfast, lunch, and dinner. No TV. No VCR. No stereo. Bedtime is 8:00 P.M. You will live like this for one week, at which time we will evaluate whether or not you are ready to live as civilized human beings and follow the normal campus routine."

The girls said nothing. Nothing. They sat there in disbelief, and after I left Mona told me they asked, "Why are you doing this to us? Plenty of kids here have done what we did and not been punished for it. Why are you picking on us?"

"We're not picking on you," she told them. "It's just that things are going to be different around here. We're setting new standards for what is acceptable behavior."

Things were very calm around the campus the next few days. The other kids definitely took note of our new way of reacting to a riot. The Hayden girls were up at 8:00 every morning, cleaning and scrubbing throughout the day. After two days we let Lily and Helen back in, and by the end of the week Wendy returned. At that point I met with all of them. It was a short speech.

"Let's put this behind us and move on. You were the best cottage on grounds before this incident, and I believe you can be the best again. We have a lot of problems on campus, and I need you to help the other staff and me to improve things. Every one of you is intelligent and has at least one special skill. We need those skills if we're going to put this place back on the right track. I love every one of you and I want the best for you."

There was one final piece of business for me. One of the tenets of this work is that whenever there is group acting-out, it is almost certain that there are adults behind it in some way. There will always be individual adolescents behaving poorly; that is the nature of this work, that's why certain young people are sent to a residential treatment center. But when there is an incident involving a large number of young people, I always dig to find out what precipitated it and if adults were possibly behind it. This takes a little work, especially since I am loathe to drag kids into it, questioning them as to what they were told by certain staff members. But it's not impossible to find out what was going on behind the scenes.

In this case it didn't take me long to find out that two Hayden staff members had been inciting the girls while Mrs. Bartley was on vacation. These two staff members apparently believed they, and not Mrs. Bartley, should be running the cottage. They fed the girls lies about Mrs. Bartley taking their allowance money and purchasing a coffee pot with it. That's what Helen had been screaming about that night. The two counselors purposely stirred things up and left at 11:00 P.M. when their shift ended, knowing full well that only one counselor would be on duty during the overnight.

I couldn't prove any of this because I wasn't willing to take statements from the Hayden girls, but I let the two counselors know that I believed they were to blame for the riot.

"I can't prove anything," I told them, "but I believe you two were behind this. I can't fire you, but I'm transferring you to other cottages. Don't ever pull anything like this again."

They protested that they were innocent, but I walked away without even listening to their lies.

Mrs. Bartley returned from vacation and unfortunately became ill with cancer a few weeks later. Mona Warren took over Hayden Cottage and did an amazing job. A year later it was voted Cottage of the Year and Mona became Employee of the Year for the entire agency. Wendy, Lily, and Helen remained the informal leaders of the cottage, but Linda transformed them into positive leaders who exhorted their peers to follow the program and work hard in school. They all left us within the next eighteen months, which was the average stay at the campus, to return to their families or move into a neighborhood group home. They were present at the memorial service we held in our chapel when Mrs. Bartley passed away. I was with her at the hospital hours before she died, and she asked me to tell the Hayden girls how much she loved them.

"All happiness depends on courage and work. I have had many periods of wretchedness, but with energy...I pulled through them all" (Honoré de Balzac, *Eugenie Grandet,* Viking Press, 1955). Courage, work, and energy got us through that horrendous night. It was a terrible experience, but ultimately it did change the entire program for the better. The adults set a new standard of behavior for the young people in our care. They saw that, and followed.

Taking a Stand

There are times in dealing with young people when you have to do what is right, even when it is unpopular, or even dangerous. These are the times you have to break with convention, when it would be easier to look the other way, to go with the flow, but something in you will not allow you to do so. For parents, this might be something as simple as forbidding a child to attend a concert or movie that you believe is inappropriate, even though "everyone else is going." Or it might be forbidding your teenage daughter from wearing inappropriate clothing, even though many of her peers dress this way.

For those of us in youth work, acting on your principles can entail even more.

At. St. Christopher's I was in charge of the campus, but the school on grounds, which all our teenagers attended, was run as a separate entity. There was a superintendent, principal, and an entire staff of teachers, guidance counselors, and educational assistants. We worked cooperatively in regard to the young people in our care, but I had no say or authority over what went on in the school.

I had been on the job only a few weeks when one afternoon one of our social workers approached me outside. She looked upset.

"Look at Kevin," she pleaded. "See what they did to him."

Kevin was a fifteen-year-old young man who I knew had suffered extreme physical and sexual abuse as a child. He was emotionally disturbed and frequently acted out in all sorts of unpredictable ways. I caught him hiding a scythe under a bush one afternoon. He'd masturbate in broad daylight in front of peers and staff. When he became upset he'd climb a tree and staff would spend hours trying to coax him down. He was one of those kids who did not really belong in a facility like ours. He belonged in a psychiatric setting, but young people like Kevin were often referred to our facility, and it could take months to get state or city officials to place them where they really needed to be.

Kevin walked over to me. I immediately noticed long bloody scrapes along his neck.

"Kevin, how did this happen?" I asked, not discounting the possibility that they were self-inflicted wounds.

"Tell him, Kevin," said his social worker.

"One of the teacher's aides did it," he said.

"Why?"

"I was fooling around in the classroom and the teacher asked me to leave, but I wouldn't. So the aide tried to force me out. He dragged me out of the classroom and onto the lawn and did this to me."

Cottage staff and school staff were all trained in how and when to physically restrain youth. There were specific circumstances when restraint was deemed necessary, essentially when the child was in danger of hurting him- or herself or others. If the restraint was done correctly, neither the child nor the staff would be harmed. There was also a specific type of counseling called the Life Space Interview that was to be done post-restraint in order to help the child to return back into program with everyone else.

Physically removing a child from a classroom because he is fooling around was not allowed. And the marks on Kevin's neck indicated to me that a proper restraint had not been performed by the teacher's aide. And it certainly didn't sound like the aide had done a Life Space Interview afterward.

I escorted Kevin over to the infirmary, which was adjacent to the school. While in there, the head nurse, Susan Knowles, told me that one of our staff members, Virginia Smith, had happened to be looking out the window when the incident occurred. She had seen the whole thing but was apparently reticent to tell me or anyone else about it.

I couldn't blame her. During my short time at St. Christopher's I had learned that some of the teacher's aides routinely beat our young people and verbally abused them at every turn. Word was that any adult who dared to turn them in would suffer the same. And the principal of the school basically protected them, acquiescing in their method of dealing with troubled young people.

I found Virginia Smith a few minutes later.

"Will you tell me what you saw?" I asked her.

"I don't really want to," she replied. She looked frightened.

"Listen, Virginia, something bad happened to this boy. They may have covered this stuff up in the past, but I am determined to put a stop to it. I really need you to tell me what happened."

She paused but then spoke.

"Well I just happened to be looking out the window of the infirmary. I saw one of the teacher's aides dragging Kevin out of the school building, and the aide just threw him on the ground and started choking him. I couldn't believe it, it was really frightening. Eventually the aide got off of Kevin and walked away. Kevin lay there for a few moments and then got up."

"And that was it?" I asked.

"Yeah, that was it, it was over."

"Thank you, Virginia," I said.

"What are you going to do with this?" she asked.

"I'm not sure," I said, "but I think I'm going to call it in to the State Child Protective Services (CPS) unit."

I and every person working on the campus and in the school was a "mandated reporter" of child abuse. If any of us saw or knew about abuse or neglect of a child, we were legally bound to report this to CPS by calling their 800 number. The staff there would then decide whether or not to investigate the incident by sending a caseworker.

It all sounds very clear-cut, but calling in an abuse allegation to CPS is rarely so. This was true even when I worked at Epiphany. There are times when staff must legitimately restrain a child who is in danger of hurting him- or herself or others, yet as a supervisor of mine once advised me, "A restraint never quite goes the way you plan it." If a kid starts swinging and resisting, it can be very difficult for staff to place hands, arms, and legs exactly as the restraint manual prescribes. If a program director calls the hotline every time a restraint does not go exactly as planned, it is easy to end up with staff who conclude, "Hey, I'm not going to restrain any kid because I can't afford to lose my job." The program director can also end up with a population of young people who discover that they can virtually run the program and do anything they want due to staff's fear of being reported for abuse.

But this one was pretty obvious to me. There was nothing in restraint training that came close to allowing the choking of a kid. My staff member had seen it, and the marks on the boy's neck proved that something had gone wrong.

I knew I'd catch hell from the school for calling CPS. The school had a reputation for reporting these things in such a benevolent way ("Oh, there was a slight altercation between a student and a school staff member, but it was really nothing, and everybody is okay") that it had been years since CPS had even sent someone over to investigate an incident.

But I did it anyway. I notified the school principal first to tell him what I was about to do, giving him and his staff member fair warning. I could tell he wasn't pleased, but I simply explained that as a mandated reporter I had to do what I believed was correct. Our executive director, Luis Medina, was out of town, but as he told me later when he learned what transpired, "We have to get the word out to school staff that this sort of thing will no longer be tolerated. You accomplished that by making that call."

CPS did accept the case. They demanded that Kevin and the teacher's aide have no further contact with each other, so the next day Kevin was placed in another class. The State sent a case worker to investigate a few days later. He interviewed Kevin, the aide, Virginia Smith, and myself. His findings were that the aide had in fact used excessive force and should undergo "further training in the appropriate use of physical restraint." I would have liked to see the aide fired from his job, but that did not happen.

There were no more incidents like that in the school. "I'm proud of what you did," the director of the infirmary, Susan Knowles, told me. But I was proud of Virginia Smith. In my mind she was the one who provided the first-hand testimony to make this stick, and it took courage for her to do it. I took a risk, but so did she. None of the aides bothered her afterward, nor did they bother me. Eventually a new principal was brought in to run the school, and over time he dismissed those staff members who refused to treat students with the respect they deserved. But I like to think that this particular incident set the stage for sending an important message about the way young people were now to be treated—without violence, coercion, or threat, and with dignity and respect.

Saving One Another

Young people are capable of incredible acts of compassion, courage, and self-sacrifice. I know this flies in the face of how they are often presented in the media—narcissistic, shallow, self-absorbed—but I have seen otherwise.

Those of us who teach, coach, and minister to youth can easily fall prey to the notion that we can single-handedly save a young person who is struggling and in need. Yes, adults can do much, but sometimes the best approach is to allow events to progress in such a way that the adolescents themselves are the agents of change for their peers who are suffering.

It was rare for the work phone in my house to ring in the early hours of the morning. It usually rang in the middle of the night, with a staff member requesting me to come next door to handle a crisis. So when I sat in my kitchen sipping coffee at 8:00 A.M. one December morning, and heard the work phone ring, I wondered what new kind of calamity awaited me on the other side of the six-foot fence that separated my personal life from my work.

I picked it up and heard a breathless voice on the other end.

"Mr. Redmond, it's me, Teasley."

Alan Teasley was one of the senior staff at St. Christopher's. He managed one of the girls' cottages.

"You know that new girl Corinne? The one who's supposed to be suicidal? She just ran out the back door of the cottage and went AWOL. She headed down the ravine."

The ravine—it was a hundred-yard thicket of vines, fallen trees, rotting trunks, and branches that sloped down at a very steep angle. Raccoons, which kids and staff frequently claimed were rabid, nested there. To the kids in our program, all of whom hailed from inner-city pockets of poverty, that ravine represented what the Atlantic Ocean represented for fifteenth-century European explorers—territory filled with all kinds of mysterious creatures that could inflict pain and suffering.

The staff wasn't comfortable about traversing the ravine either, and for that reason our kids knew an AWOL via the ravine was very effective. (The technical term is "unauthorized departure from grounds" but kids and staff alike used the vernacular AWOL.) They realized that very few staff members were going to chase a fleeing teenager down and through the ravine. If a kid was brave enough to go down there, chances were he or she was home free, or at least free to walk along the railroad tracks in the direction of the local train station. Once there, it was no big deal to hop a train into New York City, duck the conductor for the thirty-minute ride, and go AWOL.

Kids AWOLed from our program for a variety of reasons. Some left to go into town for a few minutes to buy cigarettes or junk food. Others just wanted a short break from our rules and from staff telling them what to do. But the most common reason a kid went AWOL was to return to his or her home neighborhood. As nice as St. Christopher's was, situated on the banks of the Hudson with a spectacular view of the Palisades, few of our teenagers wanted to be there. They wanted to be back in their communities, with their families and their friends. The problem was that many of these kids had been removed from their families due to neglect or abuse on the part of their parents. Or the opposite could also be true—parents had requested court assistance to get their kids out of the house and neighborhood because of their dangerous behavior. Other kids had committed and been convicted of crimes and sent to our facility as an alternative to a lock-up. Either way, these kids were now legally assigned to us. It was our job to keep them on our grounds, and if they somehow got out, it was our job to get them back.

One method of AWOLing was to walk right out our front gate. Ours was not a locked facility. There was no barbwire. There were no guards with weapons patrolling our perimeter. But there were always a few staff outside, so a teenager trying to exit through the front and out onto the street would almost certainly be stopped. If that staff member was unsuccessful in convincing the adolescent to reconsider his or her decision, other counselors would be summoned to help in the convincing. It usually worked.

But Corinne selected the ravine as her method of AWOL this bright and freezing cold December morning, and what lay at the bottom of the ravine was what frightened me the most: train tracks. Metro North and high-speed Amtrak trains ran on those tracks. And beyond the tracks was the Hudson River. Corinne definitely had a history of suicide attempts. I had skimmed her psychological and psychiatric profiles when she had arrived a few days earlier. She was fifteen years old and had endured sexual abuse for several years from her mother's live-in boyfriend. Her mother didn't believe her. Corinne then lived with different relatives, then the streets, and then a psychiatric hospital after she tried to cut her wrists. Placement in the foster care system ensued, followed by more suicidal gestures and hospitalizations, and then she was deemed safe enough to be referred to our facility.

Mr. Teasley continued: "Mark, you'd better get over here." Chances were that Corinne would reach the bottom of the ravine and do what every other kid choosing this method of AWOL did—walk to the train station and head home from there. But what if she didn't? What if she was thinking of throwing herself on those tracks or in the river?

I put on an overcoat and sprinted from my house, I unlocked the gate that separated my yard from my work, and headed across the grounds toward Mr. Teasley's cottage. I spotted him behind it, on the edge of the ravine, pointing.

"That's where she went. Right in that direction."

I peered into the ravine but could not see any kind of path that would lead me through it. I took a few steps down, unsure of how to even begin. I felt my footing give way.

"I think the kids go down it backwards," he said. "They grab the vines and lower themselves down."

Rappelling. These urban teenagers had figured out how to rappel themselves out of our program. Very innovative, but it didn't surprise me, for these kids usually were. I turned myself around and headed down the ravine butt-first, clutching vines wherever I could find them. I made slow progress. Mr. Teasley watched me, but then left, shouting, "I'll try to round up some kids to help you."

It took me about ten minutes to reach the bottom of the ravine. I was now level with the train tracks and the river, which was almost completely frozen over. I did not see Corinne. Now in my path lay a seven-foot high concrete wall Amtrak had recently constructed. I had to somehow scale that wall to see if she was on the tracks or in the river.

I stood there trying to figure out how to get over that wall, when I heard some shouting and voices behind me. I turned around and looked back up the ravine. I was absolutely stunned when I saw about a dozen of our boys, ages thirteen to fifteen, rappelling down. Mr. Teasley had apparently recruited them. "Here comes the cavalry," I said to myself.

They made it down the ravine in about one-fifth the time it had taken me. The first one down, Ted, ran over to me. He was fifteen, a tall and slender African American; he ended up at our place because of a nasty habit of beating up teachers in his Bronx high school.

"Where is she, Mr. Redmond?"

I told him I didn't know.

"How about the train station?" Ted asked. "Do you think she headed for the train station?"

"I guess that's possible, but my main concern is the Hudson River. I need to get a closer look but I'm not able to get over this wall."

The rest of the boys were with us now. Ted barked out orders.

"Guys, let's break up into teams. You four head south for the Hastings train station. You three guys come with me and we'll go north to the Dobbs Ferry station. Jaquan and the rest of you—help Mr. Redmond over that wall so he can search the river."

They did exactly as he ordered. In staff trainings we often talked about how teenagers in an institution form their own informal power structure, with one of them assuming the role of "leader" who is then supported by two or three "lieutenants." I guess I lucked out that Ted was the leader of this group and he happened to now be part of my mission.

The boys followed me to the concrete wall and boosted me over. My plan was to do a quick solo inspection of the river to see if I could spot Corinne. However, when I landed on the other side of the wall I looked back up and saw Jaquan coming over to join me. I considered ordering him back over; it was not exactly a safe spot where we now stood, with trains whizzing by every few minutes. He was a teenager and I was responsible for his safety. But once he landed beside me I figured I could use his help searching for Corinne.

We had six sets of tracks to cross to get to the riverside. We first allowed a train to pass and then made a run for the river.

Once there, we climbed onto some rocks jutting out into the Hudson. At that close range I could see that the frozen-over Hudson River wasn't actually so frozen over. Instead, large sheets of ice bobbed on the surface, producing a strange crunching sound as they ground into each other.

We spent a few minutes peering out at the river but didn't see Corinne, so we crossed back over the tracks. We went back to the concrete wall, which Jaquan easily scaled without any sign of struggle. He didn't even require a boost from me. He was in excellent shape, one of our best athletes, but a quiet, somber kid who rarely smiled. I didn't know why he had been placed in our facility, and I had no real relationship with him. We knew each other's name and that was about it. I was now by myself and tried to duplicate Jaquan's feat, leaping in an effort to get back over the barrier. I managed to get my arms on top of it, but then I hung there, panting, fruitlessly trying to pull the rest of my body over. I was embarrassed and a little anxious. Then I looked up and saw Jaquan's face. He looked down at me, the same grim look he wore every minute of every day. Without a word and displaying no emotion whatsoever, he reached back over the wall with his right arm and literally yanked me over the top. I was amazed at his strength. I felt humbled and grateful, thanking him for saving my sorry butt, and he mumbled something back.

There was nothing to do now but for me, Jaquan, and the rest of our team to climb back up the ravine and wait to find out if the other boys had found Corinne at one of the train stations. The boys scaled right up the ravine while I huffed and puffed, vowing to join a health club if and when I ever made it to the top.

I of course did make it, ran back to my house, and jumped in my car. I didn't have to drive very far. I spotted the contingent of boys we had dispatched to the Dobbs Ferry train station, walking along the street, headed back toward our

THE GOODNESS WITHIN

program. And Corinne was with them. I relaxed for the first time since receiving that call from Mr. Teasley. Her intention was apparently exactly as I had suspected from the start—to AWOL from our facility. One boy held her hand and one had his arm around her shoulder. Everyone looked calm, including her. I obviously couldn't hear what they were telling her, but I suspected the conversation was something like, "It's better to stay here and work out your problems than to go AWOL....There are some good staff here you can talk to and trust." I knew they were counseling Corinne in a way that was more effective than I or any of our social workers and psychologists could at that moment.

Once I knew the boys had Corinne back safely, I returned home, showered, dressed, and went to my office just as I would any other day. I alerted our head clinician as to what had occurred so she would be sure to have someone see Corinne, and I instructed Mr. Teasley to assign someone to stay one-on-one with her, around the clock. I spent the rest of that day doing what I always did—attending meetings, reviewing budgets, and other administrative duties. In the back of my mind, however, I was trying to think of some way to reward those boys who had willingly put themselves at risk to help one of their peers. One of the principles I learned and in which I thoroughly believed was to reward positive behavior in as concrete and public a way as possible. I frequently stated this to staff in trainings. "If a young person does something well, no matter how small or seemingly insignificant, recognize it, reward it, and shout it out loud. Build on a youth's strengths, not on weaknesses."

I decided that that night I would host a "Dinner for Heroes," inviting Mr. Teasley and the boys who had come to Corinne's (and my) rescue. I made a reservation at a local restaurant called Doubleday's, an inexpensive establishment comparable to a TGI Friday's. I called the cottages in which the boys resided and instructed staff to bring them to my office instead of the dining room at 5:00 P.M. When they arrived, I led them to one of our vans. "Where are we going, Mr. Redmond?" one of them asked. "Not far," I replied. It took us minutes to reach the restaurant, and when everyone exited the van I pointed to Doubleday's. "Go right in, guys." We walked in to find a long table for thirteen all laid out with plates, silverware, and candles. I'll never forget their reaction; they looked like they were in heaven. One boy wheeled around and asked me, "This is for us?" They couldn't believe it. These were kids who were very familiar with poverty, foster care, and homelessness. McDonald's was fine dining to them.

We sat down and the waiter handed out laminated menus listing different types of hamburgers, chicken dishes, grilled shrimp, and similar dishes. One of the boys turned to me and asked, "What's the limit?"

"What do you mean?"

"You know, what's the most expensive thing we're allowed to order?"

I was taken back by his question. I didn't grow up in a wealthy family, but when my parents took us out to a restaurant we ordered what we wanted. It was so strange and sad to think that a young man's first question would be about the price limit. "Order what you want," I told him.

"This is like the Super Bowl of eating!" exclaimed the young man next to him.

All of us ordered and in a little while the entrees appeared. I became puzzled when I noticed waiters placing two plates of hamburgers in front of some boys, along with the fries, lettuce, tomatoes, and everything else one receives when ordering a burger in a restaurant like this. I began to ask these young men, "What exactly did you order?"

"Two cheeseburgers, Mr. Redmond." I immediately realized they were ordering here as they would at a McDonald's or Burger King. I quietly chuckled at their lack of familiarity with the ordering norms at a real restaurant. I started to instruct them how this was not the way things were done at a nonfast-food restaurant, but then I refrained. Let them enjoy themselves.

Every young man there ate every single thing on his plate, including those who had ordered double portions. I recall a great deal of laughter and camaraderie throughout the meal. We recounted the day's heroics, with each person describing in vivid detail his version of what had transpired. I then clinked on my water glass, stood, and asked for attention. That afternoon I had printed "Official Hero" certificates on my computer, with each youth's name listed on his individual certificate. I called each boy to the head of the table, shook his hand, and gave him his certificate as everyone applauded. I gave one to Mr. Teasley too. He looked as happy and grateful as the boys.

The waiter returned and asked if we were interested in desert. All eyes shifted to me. "Sure." It was back to the Super Bowl of eating: sundaes, shakes, chocolate mud pies. When everyone was finished I paid the check and we piled back into the van. We traveled about a hundred yards when we came upon a deli.

"Please, Mr. Redmond, can we go in and get something to eat. We have some money of our own."

I pulled over and let them out, reminded but still amazed at just how much teenage boys could put away in one evening.

The next day several teachers and counselors told me, "The only thing those boys talked about all day was their dinner last night. It was the talk of the school."

The average stay at our campus was eighteen months. Corinne only remained a few weeks longer, managing to suc-cessfully AWOL in the middle of the night by crawling out her window and departing, we think, via the street. We never heard from her again. Jaquan, the young man who helped me search the Hudson River for her, was transferred a few months later to a group home, a positive move for him. Ted, the leader of the cavalry that morning, stayed with us the full eighteen months, exhibiting occasional emotional outbursts. Eventually the outbursts dimmed in intensity and the span between them lengthened, so we sent him home to his mother. He came back to see us a year after that, a good sign because it is usually only the kids who are doing well who come back to visit. He gave me a big hug when he entered my office. As for the other ten boys— I can scarcely remember who they were that day, much less how they fared in the long run. I do know this though: "If one has only one good memory left in one's heart, even that may be the means of saving us" (Dostoyevsky, *The Brothers Karamazov*). It is my hope that the good they did that day will remain in their hearts, and in the heart of Corinne, in order to save them all.

Creating Memories

The late Fr. James Harvey, who worked with troubled teenagers in New York City, once told a television interviewer, "Youngsters come in, they don't have food, they don't have clothes, many of them don't have a place to sleep. And people say, 'What is the one biggest thing they don't have?' And I believe it's memory. These young people have no good memories of the past."

Fr. Harvey was right. It is important to create good memories for young people, to take the time to be with them and do things with them that they will enjoy and remember forever. It is not the money you spent on your children that they will remember; it is the time you spent on them, the attention you gave them, and the interest you showed in their lives. This is what they will remember, this is what will have an impact on them.

As the fox told the Little Prince, "It is the time you have devoted to your rose that makes your rose so important....Men have forgotten this truth, but you must not forget it" (*The Little Prince,* Antoine de Saint-Exupéry, Harcourt, 1943).

The school at St. Christopher's ran a work-study program for some of our youth who were having an exceptionally difficult time academically or behaviorally. They attended morning classes, and then in the afternoon they worked with our building and grounds unit that was renovating our cottages. This gave them the opportunity to learn marketable skills like carpentry, sheetrocking, basic electrical and plumbing, and painting.

Four young men were in this program when I arrived at St. Christopher's. They were supervised in the afternoons by Tom Hughley, the head of our building and grounds department. Tom was about my age, in his mid-thirties, and he confessed to having been a little wild in his teenage years, thus believing he could relate with the boys. He was right. He took them under his wing and showed them how to hammer a nail, cut two-by-fours, use a skill saw, measure siding, prime a ceiling, and plaster patch a wall. They never acted out. They never missed an afternoon. They didn't give him lip. In fact, Tom had an Irish temper (something I know about) and would sometimes give them lip. But they handled it well, and I would always follow up by counseling Tom, "You're doing a great job with them but you have to watch how you speak to these guys...." He always accepted my advice, shaking his head, saying, "I know, Mark, I know. I'll be careful next time, I promise."

One day Tom called me with an idea.

"Open your calendar, Mark. Circle the weekend of February 21. We're taking the boys skiing."

"Skiing? These kids?"

"Sure, they'll be fine. My family has a house about five hours away, in Syracuse, and we'll have the place to ourselves. Labrador Mountain is not far from there, a good place for them to learn. We'll leave on a Friday afternoon and return on Sunday. It'll be me, you, Roy Larkin (his assistant on the building crew), and the four boys."

I told Tom I'd think about it. My main reservation was that kids at our program often behaved well in a controlled environment like ours, but when taken from that environment they could quickly display some of the behaviors that landed them there in the first place. I had had some positively disastrous off-site experiences in my years of doing this work. Tom's background was in construction, and so was Roy's. I was the only one with the training and experience to handle whatever outbursts or emergencies might occur. I also knew I'd have my six-year-old son with me on the weekend Tom suggested, so he'd be going along as well. Things were becoming more complicated than I liked, and to top it all off I had skied only a few times in my life and didn't really enjoy it.

"Mr. Redmond, I hear we're going skiing! We can't wait, this is great!"

It was Leon, a fourteen-year-old resident of our program who was on Tom's crew. Leon grew up in Jamaica and still had a thick accent. He came to America about three years ago and was living with his mother and two younger brothers in Queens. His father was nowhere to be found, which unfortunately was the case for 90 percent of the kids at our program. Leon had been truanting from his neighborhood school, generally spending his days smoking dope with the wrong crowd. His mother couldn't stop him, so she became desperate and went to Family Court. The judge there ordered him to our facility, where he had been living for the last seven months. I had to get in his face once because he didn't like the woman running his cottage and was prone to cursing her out; she had the audacity to demand that he do things like make his bed, clean his room, and do house chores. He pretty much straightened out after that and was doing well under Tom's tutelage.

"Yes Leon, we're thinking about going skiing some weekend." I guessed that Tom had told him.

"Well me, Wilfredo, Chevy, and Keenan, we all really want to go."

So all four of them knew? I guess we were now going.

Friday, February 20 arrived and that afternoon at around 3:00 P.M. I signed out a program van, threw my stuff in the back, and went looking for Tom and Ray.

"We're not driving up with you, Mark," said Tom. "I have some things I have to do at home first, but we'll follow you there about three hours later."

Oh great.

"There's plenty to see around Syracuse," he continued. "We'll see you at the house between 10:00 and 11:00."

I picked the boys up at their cottages and then we stopped by my son's elementary school to get him. Despite having divorced parents, he was a happy kid (still is) and he bounded into the van with a smile on his face, anticipating a grand adventure. I introduced him to each of the boys and off we went.

Getting to Syracuse took every bit of five hours. The trip was uneventful except for frequent disputes I had with the boys over music. They wanted me to play rap tapes they brought with them, but every one I played contained obscene language, which I had no interest in hearing and did not want my son to hear either. After ejecting about five different tapes from the cassette player, I agreed to tune in to a rap station on the radio. Halfway to Syracuse the only stations we could pick up played country, but by then the boys and my son were snoozing. I drove in silence.

We reached Syracuse, ate pizza, walked around a mall, and made our way to Tom's family's house. He had given me the key. It was a small one-story home in a post-World War II development. The snow was piled high. The driveway was plowed, but the snow covered the hedges, the mailbox, and everything else shorter than three feet. It was incredible. I remembered the Northeast blizzard of 1978 and the drifts it created, but this seemed even worse. For residents of Syracuse it was probably standard winter fare.

Tom and Roy showed up later, people were assigned beds, sleeping bags, and couches, and we all went to sleep quickly.

When I woke up the next morning, my throat was scratchy and my son told me he had no interest in learning to ski.

"You and Roy are on your own with the boys," I told Tom. He was fine with that. He dug out ski overalls for everyone and then turned to me.

"Where are their gloves and hats?"

"I don't know," I replied. "I told them to bring whatever they had."

"I'll check each guy as we drive to the mountain," said Tom, "and if we need to stop and pick up a pair of gloves or a hat we'll do it at a roadside shop."

The boys loved parading around the house in their skiwear. Like all teenagers, they were fashion conscious, and I could tell they just thought this was the best.

"What do you think, Mr. Redmond?" asked Wilfredo, a fourteen-year-old Hispanic boy. "Do I like good or what?"

"Yes, Will, you look good," I replied with a grin.

I handed Tom $250 in cash. "This should cover lift tickets, lessons, and ski rentals. In fact, it should cover two day's worth, so hang on to what's left because we'll need it for tomorrow." The boys piled in the van with Tom and Ray, and my son and I waved goodbye.

I figured I now had about ten hours to kill until they returned. I started to straighten up the house a bit as my son watched Saturday morning cartoons. I planned to hang out there for a few hours, then go out for lunch, go ice skating, hit a book store, things like that. I had a special present for the boys when they returned from skiing: tickets to the Syracuse vs. Providence basketball game that night.

About forty minutes later the phone rang. It was Tom.

"Mark, we have a little problem."

"What is it, Tom?"

"Well it's not an emergency or anything like that. Everyone's okay."

"Are they on the slopes yet?" I asked. "Did you sign them up for lessons?"

"We haven't made it that far," he responded. "In fact, we haven't even made it to the mountain yet."

"You haven't made it to the mountain? Where the heck are you?"

"We stopped at a ski equipment place like I told you we would. We went inside and I told the boys to get what they need. I guess I wasn't really watching them and what they were buying. I told them to just bring their gear up to the cash register."

"And, and, and," I interrupted.

"Well, all the money you gave me is gone. They spent it on hats, gloves, scarves, visors, things like that."

"What?????"

"Calm down, Mark, calm down. I have my credit card with me and I'll use that for the lift tickets, lessons, and rentals. We'll be all right."

"Tom, that money was supposed to last us two days! Are you crazy? How could hats and gloves for four boys cost that much?"

"They bought hats with bells and tassels on them, Bolle visors, Olympia gloves, some really nice stuff. I wasn't really paying attention to what they were getting until the lady at the register gave me the bill."

"Tom, you have to watch these kids. You can't just let them go hog wild in a store like that. You tell them I'm pissed, and they're going to have to answer to me when they get back."

I went back to picking up around the house, but I was now in a foul mood. An hour later the phone rang again. Tom.

"Mark, we have another problem."

"Are they skiing yet, Tom?"

"No, but all the equipment is rented and everyone's ready to go."

"But..."

"But my credit card is over the limit. Can you tell this woman at the register your credit card number, and then we'll all be set."

Through clenched teeth I did it.

No more calls came through the rest of that day. My son and I puttered around, going skating, eating pizza at Chuck E. Cheese's, and watching TV. At around 6:00 P.M. the skiing crew returned, and they were elated.

"We loved it, Mr. Redmond, we loved it!" They were laughing, teasing each other, telling one tale from the day after another.

"You should have seen Chevy, Mr. Redmond," said Leon. "One time he came off the ski lift and fell down right in front of it. They had to stop the lift until he got out of the way!"

"You should talk, Leon," said Keenan, another one of the boys. "I saw you run right over the instructor's skis when we were taking our lesson. Remember?"

They went on and on like this, telling stories and laughing. Roy had taken a videocamera to the slopes and filmed their many escapades. He popped the tape into the VCR in the living room, and we watched the boys trying to ski.

"There I am, look!"

"That's me, that's me making that turn, see?"

"Look at Wilfredo wipe out!"

"You have to go with us tomorrow, Mr. Redmond," said one of them. That's when I delivered the bad news.

"No one's going skiing tomorrow."

"Why not?" asked Chevy, a small skinny thirteen-year-old African American kid with a mouth full of braces.

"You guys blew all the money we had on stuff like this," I replied as I held up one of the Bolle visors. "You wasted money on that so now we don't have enough to go skiing tomorrow." I hated to be the spoiler at the big party, but I felt I had an important point to make. I waited for the cursing and threats to start, but to my surprise they took it well, heading off to take showers in preparation for dinner and the Syracuse game later on.

When we reached our seats in the Carrier Dome, the boys sat silently. I didn't have the sense they were mad at me; they were just plain exhausted. When we arrived home all except Keenan went right to bed. Keenan wanted to stay up and watch *Saturday Night Live,* as did I, because Arrested Development, a very popular group at the time, was the musical guest. Keenan had been at St. Christopher's for over a year, longer than even I had been there. He was African American, age fifteen but looked older, with a stubble of beard framing his face. People warned me about him when I arrived at the program; he was supposed to be a real troublemaker, with a penchant for sneaking off grounds, getting drunk, and becoming violent. But I hadn't seen that. To me he was a quiet, sullen kid. He actually seemed depressed much of the time, and when I read up on his background I found out why. He had no mom, and the man he was sure was his father repeatedly denied that fact, disavowing in Family Court any responsibility for Keenan. Despite his quiet demeanor, he was popular with the other kids at our facility. They looked up to him, and when a potential crisis loomed such as a big fight, I could count on him to be the voice of reason among the kids.

We watched television together, and when the band came on and sang what was their hit single at the time, "Mr. Wendell," Keenan was obviously delighted. "Watch the old guy in the band, Mr. Redmond, watch how he dances when he sings." It was gratifying for me to see a boy who was usually so quiet become so excited. The song ended and a commercial came on. Keenan was still staring at the screen when he said, "Today was the most fun I ever had."

I looked at him. "You mean since you've been at St. Christopher's?"

He didn't look back but still gazed at the TV.

"No, I mean in my entire life. This was the most fun I ever had in my entire life."

On the spot, right then and there, no matter what the cost, despite how the boys had blown $250 on fancy hats and visors, I reversed myself and decided we were going skiing again the next day. If this was the best day a fifteen-year-old had ever had in his entire life, and who knew when we'd ever be back up here again, it was worth spending a few more bucks. I left Keenan and found Tom and Roy still awake in their room.

"Let's get up early in the morning and take the boys skiing again," I said. They looked at each other and shrugged. "Okay."

Roy, Tom, and I roused the boys from their beds early the next morning. "Come on guys, up and at 'em, we're hitting the slopes again today." Each of them had a combined look of sleepiness and surprise on their faces.

"I thought you said we weren't going again," said Wilfredo.

"I changed my mind," I said. "Now are you getting up and going with us or what?"

"I am, I am," he replied as he hopped off the couch and began gathering his things.

This time I went with them. I couldn't stand the thought of hanging out in the house another day, and I wanted to see for myself all the fun they were having. I was put in charge of standing at the base of the mountain with the videocamera and filming the guys as they skied down. Tom and Roy took turns watching my son, who was delighted to find some videogame machines in the ski lodge.

It was fun watching the boys learn how to ski. After one day on the slopes they all thought they were Franz Klammer and came barreling down the mountain. They were constantly falling down, crashing into drifts and crashing into each other. At one point Chevy and Leon collided and started swinging their poles at each other. Thankfully Roy stepped in and broke it up. At one point a man noticed I was filming them and asked me, "I've been watching these kids for a while. Are they alright, I mean are they mentally off or something?"

"They're fine," I assured him, "they're fine. This is just their first time skiing."

By 4:00 P.M. my son was getting restless, and I knew we had a long ride ahead of us. I told the boys it was time to head in and return their skis.

"One more time down, Mr. Redmond, please," they asked.

"This is what it was like yesterday," said Tom. "We practically had to drag them off the slopes. They skied until the moment the lift shut down."

We let them have one more run.

That night we stopped at a family-style restaurant we found off the highway while traveling home. Like everything else that weekend, I just kept taking out the credit card. We had a really nice meal together, seated at one long table. The boys were still telling ski stories, proud of what they had achieved, teasing each other over spills and gaffes. It occurred to me sitting there watching them that for a bunch of boys who really had no families, this might be as close as they were ever going to get to be part of one.

All the boys and my son slept during the ride home. When we arrived I dropped each boy at his cottage, and each thanked me profusely for the weekend as he exited the van. The next day the whole campus was abuzz with tales of the ski trip as the videotape made its way from cottage to cottage.

At St. Christopher's we were unable to track kids and keep statistics on how they fared after leaving our program. It's something I wanted to do, but with over seventy kids in the program at any one time, and an average length of stay of eighteen months, we'd need a full-time staff person just doing that. Unfortunately, there was never the money for that. We were chronically short on funds to provide even the basics in terms of staffing. Kids left us, sometimes they kept in touch and let us know how they were doing, but often they did not.

All four of the boys on the ski trip left our program within a year. Chevy moved on to one of our neighborhood-based group homes, which was a good move for him. The braces came off, he grew about a foot, started lifting weights and before we knew it he was the star of his high school wrestling team. He worked evenings and weekends at a diner and saved every penny he earned. Then he became involved with a cult. They took all his money, then Chevy had a nervous breakdown and ended up in a psychiatric hospital. He recovered, eventually graduated from high school, was accepted into college, and lived in a dorm. He stayed at the group home during holidays and the summer. Not a bad ending. Wilfredo moved back with his family in the Bronx; we never heard from him again so I have no idea how things worked out in his life. Leon moved back with his mother in Queens. Two years later I learned he was shot and killed. I was unable to find out the circumstances of his death. I felt very badly because he was turning into a nice young man with a lot of promise. And Keenan, the kid who without realizing it got his pals back on the slopes for one last day, moved into a group home run by another agency in New York City. The following January he called me out of the blue.

"Mr. Redmond, are you taking kids skiing again this year? Can I go even though I don't live there any more?"

I chuckled. "Sure, Keenan, if we go you can come along. Give me your number and I'll call you if we make plans."

But we never did make plans. Tom left St. Christopher's to go work elsewhere, and the winter passed before Roy and I had a chance to put a trip together. We didn't go skiing that year, nor in the following years. I regret that, but I take satisfaction in the thought that we did, in the words of Fr. Harvey, create at least one good memory for those young men that weekend in Syracuse, New York.

Connections

It is important to figure out ways of connecting with your teenager. As one parent told me, "You have to find things that you both can get excited about." It is one of the ways a relationship is built. Creating a loving, caring relationship is partly talking, but it is also doing.

Whenever I started in a new job working with young people, I searched for my "vehicle," my way to connect with them. When I became director of the Epiphany Youth Hostel, I played touch football with the kids. When I later ran a group home in Bushwick, Brooklyn, for boys ages nine to eleven, I played street hockey with them in a school lot across the street. I was always searching for some way to relax and have fun with them. It couldn't be all about school, study, counseling sessions, and following rules.

Adults sometimes assume that a teenager will have no interest in doing these things with you or will be embarrassed to be seen with them. Nothing could be further from the truth. The young men at Epiphany begged me to play football with them. One boy there once said to me, "You're different from other program directors." I asked him why, and he replied, "Because you play football with us." Playing touch football constituted about one percent of my time at Epiphany, but in the mind of that teenager, and I suspect in the minds of the others there, it was the most significant thing I did. That I fundraised $X for the program, balanced the budget, met all state and city regulations, and trained the staff paled in relation to the fact that every once in a while I played football with them.

The time that you spend with your child, doing things together, is what will stand out in his or her mind. Not the fact that you earned a certain salary. Not the fact that you manage the household budget properly. Not that you serve a nutritious meal every day. Yes, these things are important. You have to do them. But what will really make a difference to your teenager is the time you spend with him or her.

When I arrived at St. Christopher's in 1992, I knew I once again had to find my vehicle, my way to connect with the kids there. Within a few weeks I noticed a dirt bicycle path that ran parallel to our campus, across the street. One Saturday morning I took out on my mountain bike to investigate. I headed north on it; it continued for several miles, running parallel to the Hudson River. People jogged on it, rode bicycles, hiked. It passed through the towns of Irvington and Tarrytown, ending at the historic Lyndhurst Mansion. It was a beautiful, scenic path. I found out it was called "The Aqueduct" because underneath it were tunnels that once carried water from upstate reservoirs into New York City.

I continued to bike on the Aqueduct after work and on weekends. I enjoyed it, and I thought the kids in our program would as well. Since they were from some of the poorest neighborhoods of New York City and Westchester, none had brought a bicycle along when they arrived at our program. They usually showed up with the clothes on their back and nothing else, rarely even a toothbrush. So my first task was to get some bicycles.

Our program was always financially strapped, wondering if we would be able to pay that month's bills. We had no money for new bikes. I picked up a copy of *Bicycling* magazine and clipped out all the ads placed by bike manufacturers. I looked up the address for each and wrote the company president a letter explaining our situation and the need for donated bicycles. I sent out about twenty and waited for the responses.

Two companies wrote back—Trek and GT. Trek mailed me a water bottle with a note saying they already donated funds to several nonprofits and were not in a position to add ours to the list. GT, however, sent me six brand new mountain bikes, assembled, all the way from their headquarters in California. I was very impressed with their generosity.

I now had six bikes but seventy-two kids on grounds. I belonged to a cycling club in Westchester County that mailed a monthly newsletter to all members. I placed a blurb in the next issue asking for donations of used bicycles that were in good condition. Within the next month I had about thirty. Now we could start biking.

I purchased bike helmets and started taking kids out on the Aqueduct. We'd go after school and on weekends. They absolutely loved it. Whenever I'd walk around the campus, I would hear, "Mr. Redmond, when can I go biking with you? When are you taking us out again?" It was a constant refrain. After a while I kept a running list of which kids went so that everyone would have a turn. Kids who haven't had many nice things given to them in life have a keen sense of fairness; if it looked like I was allowing someone to go too often, I'd be sure to hear about it.

A few months later I read about the Tour d'Cure, a bicycle tour to raise money for diabetes. There were several of them listed for different areas of the New York metropolitan area, and the one in our county, Westchester, was scheduled for a Sunday morning in June. There were varying distances which one could sign up for, the shortest being fifteen miles. I thought that this would be something that the St. Christopher's kids would really enjoy. I called the tour organizers, told them about my wish that some of our kids be allowed to ride, and they agreed to waive the entrance fee. I asked our director of maintenance, Roy Larkin, if he would come with us, and he agreed. Since he had been on the ski trip with us, I knew he interacted very well with the kids. They respected and looked up to him. And the fact that he was a black belt in tae kwan do didn't hurt either; they knew not to mess with Roy.

Roy and I agreed to take four kids with us on the tour. He invited four young men who helped out on his maintenance crew. They eagerly agreed to participate. We did a few training rides during the weeks before the tour. The boys did well. Roy and I felt they were ready to handle the fifteen miles.

The starting time for the fifteen-mile course was 9:00 A.M. I asked Roy to come by the campus with his van no later than 7:30. This would give us time to load up the bikes and drive everyone to the starting point about thirty minutes away.

At 7:00 A.M. that Sunday I started knocking on cottage doors to wake kids up, but I didn't have to. All four were wide awake and ready to ride. At 7:30 we waited at the bottom of the driveway for Roy to appear. He had the keys to the gym where the bikes and helmets were stored, although I had my Trek mountain bike and Bell helmet with me.

By 7:45 Roy had still not arrived. At 8:00 I called Roy's house. No answer. The boys were getting anxious, and so was I. It was now 8:15, and still no Roy. I began to face the prospect that perhaps we weren't going to the Tour d'Cure after all and started thinking of how to deliver this disappointing news to the guys.

Then, at 8:25, Roy's van came speeding down our driveway. He screeched to a halt in front of us, jumped out, and ran to the gym. We instructed each boy to grab a bike and a helmet. We literally threw the bikes in the van and then crowded in after them. Roy offered some kind of explanation as to his lateness, which today I can no longer recall. I just remember being panicked that we wouldn't make it for the 9:00 A.M. start.

The tour was starting on the grounds of a first-rate hotel in White Plains, and Roy lead-footed it the whole way. When we reached the site we saw hundreds of cyclists lined up and ready to go. It was minutes before 9:00. Roy pulled into a parking spot, and I directed everyone to grab a bike and a helmet and head for the starting line. "You guys start. I'll register us and catch up to you on the course." I sprinted toward the tent that housed the tour organizers and explained who I was and the special circumstances by which we were allowed to ride. I was given six numbers that we were to pin to our shirts as we rode.

I ran back to the van and saw that Roy and the boys were gone, presumably now at the starting line. I heard a starting gun go off and a loudspeaker announce, "Good luck, everyone, and see you in fifteen miles." I opened the van doors to fetch my beautiful Trek and the new sleek helmet. To my astonishment, neither was there. Instead I found a beaten-up girl's three-speeder and a pink helmet with flower decals on it. The boys had taken what was mine and left me with this.

I was absolutely fuming. Here I was decked out in all the standard biking accessories—Cannondale shorts, SoBe shirt, Nike biking shoes—and I was left with this bike and helmet. I couldn't believe it. I stood there for a moment staring at the bike and the helmet. How was I going to travel fifteen miles on this?

I decided I was going to bike the Tour d'Cure no matter what, and I was going to catch up to Roy and those kids and reclaim my bike and helmet. I jumped on the bike, put on the helmet, and started peddling. To reach the start of the course I had to go past a lawn about the length of a football field, and on it were several dozen cyclists who were either race organizers or who had gone out earlier and were already back. All were dressed in Spandex biking outfits, many were women and all seemed to be in fantastic shape, limbering up and stretching out on the lawn. Only recently divorced, I was conscious about making a good impression on the women who were there that day. Instead, I cycled past them and winced, praying that no one I knew from my cycling club was there who might recognize me. It was the hardest and fastest I ever cycled to the start of a tour.

The first mile was downhill, but a slight uphill followed that. I went to switch gears and to my dismay learned that the bike was stuck in first. I was going from bad to worse. Westchester County is anything but flat, and now I'd have to do the whole fifteen miles stuck in the lowest gear. I pedaled on ahead anyway, more determined than ever to catch up to the boys.

At about the five-mile point I reached the first rest stop, and there they were. Jim, a stocky fifteen-year-old African American from Brooklyn, had my bike and helmet. He had a big grin on his face as did Roy and the others.

"Jim, I hope you've enjoyed that Trek for the last five miles," I said as I happily dismounted from the girl's three-speeder.

Jim didn't protest. He just kept grinning as we exchanged bikes and helmets. When he put on that pink helmet with the flowers, and took a few practice strokes on the bike, the other boys howled with laughter. "You look like a crazy fool!" one of them said.

By now my guilt was kicking in. Jim really did look ridiculous on that thing. So I stopped him before he cycled away.

"Give me back the bike."

He looked at me.

"Come on, Jim, take the Trek back and give me the girl's bike."

He did. I, however, kept the Bell helmet. I had to maintain some dignity for myself.

"See this crummy little bike I'm riding," I announced. "Even though I'm twenty years older than you, and I'm on this thing, I predict I will finish ahead of all of you."

"You're on," said one of the boys.

We raced for the next ten miles, and I won. Roy missed a turn and ended up on the twenty-five-mile course, so I beat even him. I crossed the finish line greeted by tour organizers who cheered and clapped. I felt triumphant and I know the four boys did too as they came in behind me. Kids who end up in a residential treatment center haven't received much affirmation in their lives. They don't have many people cheering for them. I could tell by the look on each one's face that this meant a lot.

We sat on a big lawn waiting for Roy's return, wondering just where he was. It was a sunny, gorgeous day and there was free food and drink. At one end of the lawn I spotted a line of massage tables, with masseuses offering free rubdowns to all cyclists who had finished.

"Come on, guys, this is the greatest," I told them.

"No way," they responded.

"Are you guys kidding? It's free. A massage usually costs at least $60 and they're giving them away here. Trust me, you'll love it."

They shook their heads no.

"Fine," I said. "You can watch me enjoy myself."

I lay down on one of the tables and a female masseuse came over. "Is there any area you'd like me to focus on?" she asked. I told her I had a history of lower back pain and asked if she could concentrate there. She instructed me to lie on my stomach, and then she peeled down the waist of my biking shorts an inch or two in order to be able to properly massage that area.

"Yo, Mr. Redmond, watch out, she's grabbing your butt!" said one of the boys. The other guys roared. I stretched my neck in their direction and smiled.

"Control yourselves, gentlemen, control yourselves."

Roy eventually appeared. He looked much more tired than the rest of us as he tried to figure out exactly where he had made a wrong turn. He sat down with us, ate his lunch, and like the kids he took a pass on the massage. We just lay there on that lawn for the next few hours, enjoying the music and the day, surrounded by hundreds of other cyclists who were doing the same. I had the sense that for kids who were used to neighborhoods that were violent and harsh, this was a welcome change. They were in no rush to leave and neither was I.

Eventually it was time to gather our bikes and belongings to return to the campus. I had a camera with me and asked a passerby to snap a group shot of us. He did so, and when I had it developed I sent it into the Westchester Gannett paper. They printed it later that week.

It is seven years later and I keep one copy of that picture pinned to the bulletin board in my office, and I have one at home. In fact, as I write this I am looking at it right now. It is framed and sits on the desk next to my computer. There we are—Roy, the four boys, and me—arms around each other's shoulders with a bicycle in front of us (but not the girl's three-speeder).

All of those boys departed from St. Christopher's within a year. One was accepted into Job Corps. Two of them improved enough to be able to return home to their family. But one left our campus one day and never returned; he called to say he was fine but wouldn't tell us where he had run to. He said he was tired of the program and wanted to be on his own. He was only sixteen. We never heard from him again, and I wonder how he has fared.

What Roy and I did that day was simply give those young men an experience to enjoy. They had not had much of that in their life, but they did that day. And that's what made it worth it.

Loss

When you encounter a young person who is troubled, rebellious, antisocial, disrespectful to adults, unmotivated, even filled with hatred—you would be very wise to heed the advice of Christ and, "Judge no one, lest you yourself be judged." This is because you are very likely viewing only one half of the equation. What is often hidden are all those factors leading up to such behavior: a chaotic family life; a lack of responsible, caring, and supportive adults who are positive role models; a self-image that is extremely low. These are the ingredients that produce adolescents who seem hell-bent on destruction, their own and that of the world around them.

When I finally found the South Bronx street for which I had been searching, I almost immediately spotted my destination: a funeral home. From the vantage point inside my car, it looked like little more than a storefront, wedged in between a bodega and an apartment building. Except for the sign on the window, "Wade Chapel and Funeral Home," I would have had a hard time figuring out that this is where the service for Levon's mother would take place.

None of us were surprised when she passed away. Levon, a sixteen–year-old African American, told us when he arrived at St. Christopher's that his mother had AIDS and was very ill. That was one of the reasons Levon was referred to us in the first place. A Family Court judge decided that Levon's mother was too ill to take care of him. Levon had not helped the situation by hanging out with a gang and being picked up on a weapons possession charge.

During his first few months with us we knew his mother's condition was getting worse. Levon didn't tell us much, but his social worker Vera Strand did. She also let us know that Levon's entire family was pretty much in disarray. Levon's father was a drug addict who had not played an active role in the family for years. Levon had four older brothers, two of whom were in jail. None of this fazed me; it was standard fare for the kids at our center. Our goal was to keep Levon from a similar fate.

When Vera called to tell me that Levon's mother had passed away, I asked a counselor with whom he was close to tell him the news. Levon asked for permission to go stay with his brothers for a few days until the funeral. Of course we agreed, and when I found out the date and time of the funeral I arranged my schedule to be there.

My plan was to bring with me as many of the seventy-two kids from our facility as I could. Levon was popular at St. Christopher's. He had a nice personality, smiled a lot, and could crack a quick joke. Staff generally liked him and so did his peers. I wanted them to be at the funeral as a show of support for Levon. But it didn't work out that way. There were midterms taking place at school, and then I got busy doing a hundred other things. When the time arrived to leave for the funeral I had only three kids with me, and I was angry with myself.

I parked a block away from the funeral home, and as we walked up Levon came out of a car parked in front of it. He waved us over and we shook hands. He seemed glad that we were there. He introduced us to his brothers, and I told him we'd see him inside.

The service was scheduled for 10:00 A.M., and when I entered shortly before that time I asked a chapel employee if the service would start in a few minutes. He responded yes. We sat down in a row of chairs near the back. The chapel was poorly lit and very small, able to fit perhaps only a hundred people. In front was an open casket containing Levon's mother.

Ten o'clock came and went, and at 10:15 Levon's social worker arrived. We chatted a bit, and I told her how badly I felt for not bringing all of Levon's friends from the program. People entered the room, presumably relatives and friends of the deceased. Soon it was 10:30, and the service had yet to begin. 10:45. Now I was getting antsy, and so were the three teenagers with me. I didn't even see Levon and his brothers inside the chapel. Vera volunteered to go to the chapel office to find out what was causing the delay.

She returned with a distraught look on her face.

"You won't believe this, Mark. Levon's mother was on public assistance, and when someone on PA dies the family is entitled to $1,000 for funeral costs. Well, Levon's drug addict father, who hasn't even seen his wife in years, heard she died and went down to the welfare office and picked up that thousand. Now no one can find him. Chances are he's out smoking it up right now."

I couldn't believe what I was hearing.

"The funeral director will not start the service until he has the money," she continued. "That's why we're sitting here waiting."

"Where is the director?" I asked.

She led me to his office. We walked in and discovered several of Levon's relatives speaking with him. He too was African American, a small elderly man with gray hair, dressed in a suit.

"I'm not going to start this service until I see the money," he said. "I'm just not going to do it." They pleaded with him, promising that they would try to get the money refunded from welfare later in the week and pay him then. But he wasn't buying it.

I interrupted. "How much do you need?"

He looked at me and paused for a second. "Seven hundred," he said. "Seven hundred dollars will do it."

At that point Vera grabbed me by the lapels and pulled me aside. I knew her pretty well; she was a street-smart woman who grew up and still lived in the Bronx. She pulled her face right up to mine.

"Don't do it, Mark."

"Don't do what?" I replied.

"You're thinking of writing out a check, and I'm telling you, don't do it."

She had read my mind. "But I feel terrible," I said. "I mean, this is crazy. This poor woman is dead, her crack head husband has screwed the family over, and they deserve to at least have her buried with some dignity. And the family seems to think they can get the money back from welfare."

"Don't be foolish, Mark. That money is gone, gone, gone. They will never see it again and neither will you. Do not write a personal check for this. I'm telling you, you're making a mistake."

I knew she was right, and I was not in the financial position to take a $700 hit on my checking account. So I returned to the main room, which by now was chaotic. Some people were on cell phones in an effort to dig up money. "Hey, people from my office will kick in fifty bucks," I heard someone yell. Others were walking in with food they had purchased from the bodega next door. "Who wanted the Sprite? Who asked me to buy Doritos?" The body of Levon's mother lay in state before us throughout it all.

I wanted to get out of there, so I lied and told the three kids that I had promised the school to have them back before noon. We exited the chapel and discovered Levon standing out on the sidewalk. Each of us shook his hand, explaining why we had to go. The three teenagers headed for my car, and I had a brief moment alone with Levon. He exuded an air of embarrassment combined with anguish. Staring down at the sidewalk, he shook his head. "I know I'm screwed up," he said quietly, "but you know what's scary? Compared to the rest of my family, I have it all together." I patted him on the shoulder and left, so very glad I had not invited all the other kids from the program.

Levon returned to us a few days later. He never brought up the funeral again, and neither did I. I never found out if it took place or not. I presume the latter.

I was lucky, in a way, that day. I was afforded a snapshot view of what goes on behind the scenes with young people who are troubled, who are filled with hate. That experience changed the way I look at my work. I used to spend most of my time and energy thinking about better ways of reaching and changing troubled young people. I now think more in terms of how we can support and teach parents to do a better and more responsible job of parenting. I think more about how we can create neighborhoods and communities that have the supports families need in order to overcome the obstacles they face. I think more about how to create a social and economic system that is based on the Gospel imperative to "let justice flow like water, and uprightness like a never-failing stream."

Nonviolence

Several years ago criminologists predicted a dramatic increase in violent crime in America due to a demographic increase in the number of teenagers in this country. They actually labeled them "juvenile super predators" and urged politicians to start building more prisons for the influx that was sure to come.

It never happened. In fact, the person at the forefront of this theory, John DiIulio Jr., has since apologized and became head of the White House Office of Faith-Based and Community Initiatives. (All I can say is, "The Lord loves a repentant sinner.")

I did not accept then, and I don't accept now, that violent behavior perpetuated by teenagers is inevitable. I think that even at-risk youth like the ones I work with, who have criminal histories and have belonged to gangs, can be taught to live non-violently. They can be taught to recognize and identify with the core of compassion and goodness that exists within them and within all of us. They can be taught Jesus' words about nonviolence, about not returning an eye for an eye, or a life for a life. They can be taught that as Jesus was being brutally murdered, his last plea was not for retribution, but for forgiveness, because his tormentors did not know what they were doing.

This is not pie-in-the-sky Christianity. I know first-hand the kind of violence young people can face today. Our job as adults is to teach them how to respond the right way.

"Mr. Redmond, our coach isn't here today. Who's going to drive us to the game?"

Edwin stood before me with a look on his face that asked the unspoken question, "How about you?" He was one of the young men on the basketball team we had formed at St. Christopher's a few months earlier. Edwin was our point guard, and he was good. Not that I knew much about basketball. I played football in high school, rugby in college, and was now into the more sedate and less violent sports of bicycling and tennis. Basketball was never my sport, but it was *the* sport for the young men at St. Christopher's.

"Crap," I thought to myself, silently cursing the recreation worker who once again failed to show for his shift. He doubled as our basketball coach. He knew the boys had a game that night, and he also knew how excited they were to play against other teams. I had been a big proponent of starting a basketball team when I became director. Not only was the entire institution in disarray when I arrived, but the recreation program was nonexistent. Instead of basketball hoops, someone had tied two milk crates to a wire fence, and that's what kids used for a court. It was pitiful. I knew from experience that keeping kids busy through sports was important. So we built a nice outdoor court and a few months later we registered with the county high school basketball league. We dubbed our team the Cougars; it was a sentimental choice on my part because I had played on the St. John's Cougars when in high school.

We only had thirty-six boys at St. Christopher's, and we would now be competing against high schools that often had over five hundred male students. When we had our first tryout I warned our boys about this, but it didn't matter to them. Almost all thirty-six tried out, and the dozen who made it

were issued blue and gold uniforms with "Cougars" embla-
zoned on front.

Our team was demolished the first few games, losing by
thirty or forty points. I wasn't surprised. Besides the fact that
we were competing against much larger schools, there was the
reality that the young men we played against had often been
teammates since the sixth grade; the average stay for a youth at
our facility was eighteen months. The kids at these county
schools knew each other's moves, functioned well together, and
were well coached. There was really no comparison.

But I figured we had a chance against School 19. It was
located in Yonkers, and their team was not supposed to be that
good. I didn't want to see our guys miss this game for the simple reason that our coach failed to show up.

"Okay, Edwin, I'll drive you. Get the team together and tell
them to meet me at the van in ten minutes. I just have to run
home and get my son."

Aiden was only six at the time. He had a play date with a
next door neighbor, and I didn't feel comfortable leaving him
there for several more hours. "Come on, honey, we're going to
a basketball game," I told him.

When Aiden and I arrived at the van the team was there wait-
ing for us. I could tell the guys were excited. "Maybe this time we
won't get blown out," said James, a six-foot-two African
American who was our center. Everyone piled in, including
Aiden, and I started driving away. That's when I saw Mona
Warren, our new Recreation Director. She flagged me down.

I rolled down the window.

"Mark, what are you doing? Where's Mr. Salas?"

I told her that her staff member, our coach, had once again
pulled a no-show. "I'm going to have to speak to him about
this," she said. I encouraged her to.

"Mark, are you going to coach these kids tonight?"

"Yes."

"Have you ever coached a basketball team before?" she asked.

"No."

"Do you know anything about coaching basketball, Mark?"

"I'll just wing it," I responded.

She shook her head. "Open the van, I'm coming with you."

Mona already had a lot of responsibility on her shoulders that night. I had a dozen boys, but she had to orchestrate events for the other sixty-plus kids on grounds.

"Are you sure, Mona? Don't you have a lot to do tonight?"

"Ahh, they'll be alright without me for a few hours," she answered. I didn't try very hard to dissuade her.

We arrived at School 19, which was in a low-income section of Yonkers. It looked like a fairly new facility, and I parked at the end of the block. We went in through the gymnasium entrance and ran into a thicket of kids. There was apparently another game going on. A Hispanic man came up to me and introduced himself as the coach of the team we were to play. He told me that our teams would be on the court in a few minutes.

I took my son by the hand as Mona and I led the boys into the basketball area. For a new facility it was surprisingly small. The court itself filled almost the entire area. There were no stands from which people could watch the game. Fans would have to stand alongside the court.

The School 19 players took their half of the court to practice. I watched them. They were all minority kids, mostly Hispanic. Our team was primarily African American.

The game began and within minutes we fell behind by ten points. I feared another blowout.

"I can't believe our guys don't even know the basics of playing hoops as a team," Mona whispered to me. "Now I really want to talk to Salas! What's he teaching them?"

As the game progressed we scored a few baskets but School 19 just kept widening its lead. The forty or fifty fans who lined the walls whooped and hollered, calling out to their favorite players. They were enjoying the wipeout.

At half time we were down by twenty-two points. Mona gathered the guys into a circle. She had been an All-New York City basketball player at City College a dozen years earlier. She knew basketball, she knew strategy, and most important of all, she knew how to get teenagers to follow her instructions. She laid out a few basic plays for them, changed some defensive assignments, and exhorted them to go out and be more aggressive.

And it worked. Our guys started hitting their shots, blocking School 19 shots, making steals and hitting passes. The twenty-two-point gap narrowed to eighteen, then fifteen, and then eleven. The boys were high-fiving each other all over the court, as were Mona and I. We were ecstatic. For once we were in a game. Even my little son was paying attention.

At some point near the end of the third quarter I took note of the crowd. They were no longer cheering and hollering. In fact, they looked pissed off. And then for the first time I realized that all of them were teenagers or young men who looked to be no older than age twenty. The only adults in that gym were Mona, the opposing coach, the ref, and me. I began to feel uneasy.

School 19's lead went down to seven. Five. With seconds to go in the quarter, Levon, our center, took the ball the length of the court, faked out a few defenders, feigned a pass, and slam-dunked it into the hoop. He went crazy and so did his teammates, mobbing him. I then heard a loud crash and saw a metal chair go bouncing across the court. One of the School 19 fans had tossed it.

The buzzer went off signaling the end of the third quarter. The ref grabbed the ball, held it into the air, blew his whistle, and yelled, "Game over!" I ran out onto the court.

"Game over? What do you mean, game over? That's just the end of the third quarter!"

He was a middle-aged African American man with a thick moustache and heavy sideburns. A blue tee shirt was stretched tight over his protruding belly. He stared right into my eyes and said, "Mister, if you know what's good for you, you'll end this game now while you're still losing. Don't push for a fourth quarter, believe me."

Everyone started milling about the court at this time—the angry fans, our team, their team. The opposing coach came up to me. He looked very nervous.

"Where's your van?" he asked.

"Down the block," I replied.

"I'm begging you," he continued, "please get your team in it fast and get out of here."

My heart was pounding at this point. I had my son by the hand and we headed for the exit. I grabbed some of our players as I went. I couldn't see Mona. I was hoping she had the rest of the boys and they were already outside. Aiden and I made it out the front door with six of our players in tow. We stood out on the sidewalk, but I still didn't see Mona and the other players. Within a minute I realized we were being surrounded by a gang of young people. I recognized them as School 19 fans. Then one of them smashed a glass bottle to the ground. When I heard that, I just yelled to all of our players, "RUN!" We tore off in the direction of the van. I didn't even look behind me. I just prayed the angry mob wasn't running after us. For a second my son's hand slipped out of mine. I immediately stopped, wheeled around and screamed, "Aiden! Aiden!"

"Don't worry, Mr. Redmond, I have him." It was Steven, one of our players. He had literally picked Aiden up in his arms and was carrying him like a loaf of bread as he ran.

We reached the van in about thirty seconds, and I fumbled for the key to open it. "Come on, Mr. Redmond, come on!" one of the boys implored. I found the key, opened the van and we piled in. "Lock the doors, lock the doors," I instructed them.

We were safe, but where were Mona and the other boys? I prayed they weren't still in the gym, taking a beating.

"There they are, Mr. Redmond, right there!" One of the boys pointed toward the front of the gym, where we had just been threatened. I hit the gas pedal, and one of the kids said, "Drive up on the sidewalk to get them," which is exactly what I did. We roared up to Mona and the other boys, and thank God they looked okay. They jumped in and we sped off.

I do not believe that teenage violence is inevitable, but I understand that it is going to sometimes happen. We saw it that night, and it is frightening. The challenge for me was teaching our young men two things—not to respond in kind, and to refuse to let incidents like that deter them from their goals. Even though our boys had been denied the chance at a victory that night, they shrugged it off, rose above it, stayed positive, played out the rest of the season, continued to improve their play, and even won a game—by one point, with a three-point shot at the buzzer. I was there for it, as was my son. It was a wonderful moment and wiped away the bitterness of what had occurred that night at School 19.

Learning from Failure

Several years ago I taped the Rudyard Kipling poem *If* to my son's bedroom wall. It contains many messages I believe are important for him to learn, not the least of which is, "If you can keep your head about you when all about you are losing theirs..."

Things can go wrong, sometimes very wrong, when dealing with young people. Small mishaps can compound exponentially into large mistakes that can lead to catastrophe. It is important to plan carefully, paying attention to details, stick to the plan, and if things do go awry, "keep your head about you."

At the close of my second summer as director of St. Christopher's, Mona Warren suggested a Labor Day outing at Rye Playland for all seventy-two kids. Playland was only about twelve miles away. It is the quintessential American amusement park. Ever see the movie *Big,* starring Tom Hanks? Remember the scene in which the little boy is at an amusement park and asks the "Amazing Zoltar" to transform him into an adult? That was filmed at Playland. Built in the 1930s as a WPA project, it is not very big, encompassing only a few acres. It is situated right on the Long Island Sound. There is a picnic area for barbecuing, an old-fashioned wooden roller coaster, a Haunted House, Hall of Mirrors, a video arcade, and bumper cars. There is nothing high tech about it. It's like stepping back in time to the kind of amusement park your parents used to visit.

I agreed to Mona's request, thinking that it would be a nice way to reward everyone. That summer had gone very well. We received a grant that provided every youth with an off-grounds job at a nonprofit or civic organization such as the library or a nursing home. The kids had handled this extra responsibility well. There were no riots or fights that summer. I wanted the kids to have some kind of celebration before the start of school.

I couldn't go with them to Playland because I had plans for that day, but I came on grounds that Labor Day morning to see Mona and the kids off. The dozen staff members she had assigned to the event were with her, an adequate number to supervise seventy-two youth. People packed barbecue equipment into the vans because the plan was to stay at Playland throughout the lunch and dinner hours. I waved to them as they drove off, and as I turned to go home an anxious thought popped into my mind: "What a great summer we've had—no incidents, no fights. But all seventy-two of our kids, together, in one public place? This could be risky. I hope it doesn't blow up in my face." Not that I could do anything about it; the vans were on their way to Playland. I hoped I was wrong, that I was simply overreacting.

I visited my family out on Long Island that day and returned to my house on campus at around 9:00 P.M., in time to catch the first Monday Night Football game of the season. Before settling down in front of the television, I phoned the campus administrator on duty to see how things were and if he had heard from the Playland staff. He reported that all was well and that Mona had called during the afternoon to report that everything was fine. "Great," I thought, gently chastising myself for my pessimistic thoughts earlier that day.

I began watching the game. I can't recall who was playing, but I do remember when a channel 7 reporter came on screen during a commercial break to preview the stories they'd be covering during the half-time news report.

"A riot occurred in Rye Playland this evening. Teenagers fought with the police, and several youth have been arrested. We'll have that story as well as stories about…"

My immediate thought was: "Oh my God. I hope those aren't our kids." I reached for the phone to call the campus administrator, but it rang before I could pick up the receiver.

"Mark, we have an emergency. A bunch of our kids have been arrested at Playland."

My head fell into my hands. I silently cursed myself, wishing I had listened to my own warning earlier that day.

"I'm coming right over," I told him. "Get me four of our best staff members." I got into my car, stopped at the campus, and picked them up. We headed for Playland, usually about a thirty-minute ride. I made it in twenty. None of us said much in the car. I gripped the steering wheel, grinding my teeth, picturing a dozen different scenarios of what could have happened.

I exited from the interstate onto Playland Parkway. We were the only car heading toward the park. A steady stream of vehicles passed in the other direction, leaving it. About a quarter mile from the entrance, I saw on the horizon a galaxy of spinning red police lights. It looked like every police car in the county was there, with the lights endlessly revolving. I pulled up to the entrance, hoping to drive into the parking lot, but a cop stood there and motioned me away. I rolled down my window and yelled over to him.

"Officer, I've got to get in there."

"Oh no you're not," he shot back. "There's a riot going on. No one's allowed in."

"A riot going on." His words echoed in my ears. My heart pounded. What a mess, what a freaking mess.

I parked my car on a side street and decided to leave the four counselors there while I tried to talk myself into the park. I approached the cop and explained who I was and why I was there. He let me through. I walked in and I didn't see any riot going on, but it was still chaotic. People were trying to drive out but police cars were in the way. Scores of people were waiting for buses to take them home, but the buses weren't there. I didn't even know where to start looking for our kids. Were they all locked up? If so, where? Was there a lock-up on the grounds of Playland? Where was my staff?

Then I saw Mona. She looked sick, drenched with sweat. I yelled to her. She ran over to me.

"Mona, what happened? Where are our kids? Where is the staff?"

"Mark, it was crazy. One boy started fighting with a cop and then all hell broke loose. Seven of them are arrested. I sent the rest of the kids back with the staff. They're already on their way back to campus."

"Where are the seven who were arrested?"

"I don't know. I don't know if they have them locked up here or somewhere else."

We asked a cop if he knew where the kids were. He directed us to a sergeant, who told us the seven were being transported to the county jail about a half hour away. I led Mona to my car; she crammed into my Toyota alongside the four counselors. We sped back to campus. I let the counselors off, and Mona and I grabbed a van to go to the county jail. Now was my chance to find out from her exactly what had transpired.

"Mark, the day was great. We set up our barbecue and food in the picnic area. I assigned certain staff to do the cooking and others to supervise the kids. We had lunch, we had dinner, everything was fine. We were starting to pack up to leave when

Michael Craig asked if he could carry around the boom box we had brought."

Michael was an African American youth, about age sixteen. He came from the Bronx, from an extremely dysfunctional family. There was no father in the house, there never had been. Michael's older brothers were all in jail. His mother couldn't control any of her kids, and Michael was no exception. I knew from reading his file that he had assaulted teachers in school. He had been in several foster homes growing up but had been thrown out of all of them. This was not an atypical history for youth at our program, but even acknowledging that, I knew from my own experience with him that he was a hothead with a very short fuse. I had seen him go ballistic with staff, and he even stepped up to me one time when I tried to stop him from fighting another youth. He was not one of my favorite kids.

Mona continued. "The boom box was by our barbecue all day, playing music. When we finished dinner Michael asked if he could take it with him while he walked around the park. I told him that was fine, but we were leaving in about thirty minutes.

"Next thing I know, kids are running over to me, screaming. 'Miss Warren, the cops are beating up Michael and some of the other kids. You'd better get over there.' Mark, I couldn't believe what I was hearing. Apparently a cop had approached Michael and told him to turn down his music. Michael did, but a few minutes later the cop stopped him again and asked him why he hadn't turned down the sound. Michael told the cop he did, but the cop didn't believe him. He told Michael he could either take out the batteries or leave the park. Michael said, 'I'll leave,' and then headed toward our picnic area. The cop must have wanted Michael to go in the other direction, and he grabbed him. Michael reacted by swinging. The cop took his club out. Jermaine saw this and jumped the cop from behind. Other policemen came on the scene, and they started swinging their clubs. That's when I got there. A bunch of our other kids jumped into it, so now there were about twenty white cops swinging sticks at thirty or forty black and Hispanic kids. It was nuts, just nuts. And there were all these people watching the whole thing going down, some guy was even videotaping it. Our kids just lost it, but so did the cops. It was amazing no one was shot. The police put the cuffs on Michael, Jermaine, and Monica because she supposedly bit a policeman. When the rest of our kids saw them being led off like that, in handcuffs, they acted even worse. So the cops arrested four more. It was all that our staff and I could do to keep every kid there from attacking more police."

My stomach just sunk as I listened to all this.

We reached the county jail and I spoke to the captain on duty. He informed me that they were releasing everyone to us, except for Michael and Monica. They would be held for several days. Those being released would have to appear in court later on in the week, although the captain wasn't sure what the charges would be.

Mona and I had to wait there for several hours before the five youth were released. I struck up a conversation with the captain.

"How bad will this look in the media?" I asked.

"Channel 7 has called us already," he said. "They'll be coming by. This is going to be a story."

I felt my stomach churn. Answering hard questions from reporters, the blare of camera lights—this whole thing was just getting worse and worse. I then asked him who the officers were on duty in Playland. He told me that they deploy rookie cops to patrol Playland. I asked if any were minority. "None," he answered. Now I had an even better image of what occurred and why. A force of white rookie cops, minority kids, and one hothead with a blaring boom box—a formula for disaster. Mona was right. We were lucky no one was shot.

After several hours the five kids were released to us. We piled them in the van and headed back to campus. None of them expressed any remorse for what they had done. All they wanted to talk about was the violent tactics of the white police. Jermaine practically boasted about jumping on the cop when he saw the latter grabbing Michael. Jermaine was sixteen, and very physically strong, probably the strongest in our program. African American, he was from a tough section of Brooklyn where he had been dealing drugs and running with a gang. There was no mother in his family, and his father and step-mother could not control him. He was sent to our facility, and we had scarcely little more success than they did. The girls on grounds worshipped him, despite the fact that he had a penchant for striking whomever happened to be his girlfriend at the moment.

I seethed as I listened to the kids talk. They were wrong, dead wrong, for taking on the cops as they had. I wasn't there, so I didn't know if the police had used excessive force or not. But I knew how Michael Craig could be when confronted by an authority figure, and I knew Jermaine's propensity toward violence. I was certain those two were in the wrong, and in my mind so was any youth who attacked the police to defend them. I wanted to say all this to the kids in the van, but I didn't. I was very conscious of the fact that I was a white director at a facility consisting of primarily minority staff and exclusively minority youth. And we were only one year removed from the Rodney King incident. I decided it was better to let Mona do the talking, and believe me, she let them have it.

When we reached the campus we dropped the kids off at their cottages. Mona and I sat alone in the van for a few minutes.

"Mark, is this going to cost me my job?"

I thought for a moment.

"Mona, did you see the PBS series about the Civil War recently?"

She looked at me as if I had two heads.

"No."

"Well I did, and you know what really struck me as I watched it? The truly great generals—Grant, Halleck, men like that—what made them great was not that they never lost a battle. They all lost at least one major battle, but what made them great was that after a loss they were able to pick themselves up, learn from their mistakes, and go on to win other battles. That's what separated them from other generals, who, when they experienced a loss, never really recovered.

"Mona, we're going to be like those great generals. We're going to analyze exactly what we did wrong today, learn from it, and go on to win other battles."

She looked relieved, but in my own mind I asked myself the same question: Would I lose my job?

That week I faced Luis Medina and the St. Christopher's board of directors to explain what had gone wrong. I didn't blame Mona or the kids. I blamed me. Sounds noble, but what choice did I have? I was director of the program, I was responsible. They accepted what I had to say and allowed me to keep my job.

A few days later I sat down with Mona to review step-by-step all the mistakes that led up to the incident, including why someone brought a boom box to Playland in the first place when they were banned from our campus. We established new procedures for off-grounds recreation activities, the first of which was to take no more than twelve kids to any one event.

As for the kids who were arrested, I refused to allow Michael Craig back into our program. I wanted to send a strong message to all the other kids that there was no room in our facility for someone like him. I remembered the time, when

I first arrived at St. Christopher's, that one of our boys was arrested for robbing a store with a gun while on a weekend visit to his home in Brooklyn. The kids back on campus talked about him as if he were a hero. I didn't want that to happen again, this time with Michael. He was no hero, and I didn't want him around. I discharged him to another program like ours, and I later learned he assaulted a counselor there and was arrested. I hope I am wrong, but I assume he has joined his brothers in prison.

I considered transferring Jermaine out as well. In my mind he was equally culpable. I decided against it for a very practical reason—to get the New York child welfare bureaucracy to approve an emergency transfer is almost impossible. Their attitude is, "Once you have a youth, he is yours to keep, no matter what he does. Don't ask us to move him elsewhere." I had to pull every string available to get rid of Michael; I didn't think I could do it for Jermaine as well. So we hung on to him. He was placed on probation a few weeks later, which for a sixteen-year-old in New York State is a slap on the wrist. It affected his life not one iota. He remained at our program another year and actually improved quite a bit. On his last day I asked him if he thought we had helped him at all.

"Oh yes," he replied. "I am able to talk about my feelings now and I don't hit girls anymore."

I stood there with my mouth open, marveling at just how far he had come while with us.

Monica was released to us after a few days and also received probation. The others were charged with disorderly conduct.

We never had an incident like the Playland one again. Two years later I nominated Mona Warren for Employee of the Year, and she won. A year later she was named Youth Worker of the Year by the Child Welfare League of America.

"Nothing fails like success because we don't learn from it. We learn only from failure" (Kenneth Boulding). What happened at Playland that day was a total failure, a disaster. Yet we learned much from it. The seeds for future success were sown there.

Faith and Change

I once heard a talk by a priest, who was also a clinical psychologist, in which he said, "If you are a Christian, you have to believe that people can change. If you don't believe people can change, you have no right calling yourself a believer in Jesus Christ and in his gospel message. It's as simple as that." I have remembered these words many times during my years working with young people.

It is imperative that parents and those who teach or minister to youth have a deep conviction that change is possible. We must believe that because a person has acted one way for most of his or her life does not mean he or she is destined to act that way forever. We must believe in the power of God to act dramatically and forcefully to change people's lives for the better.

Jeremy was only fifteen when he arrived at St. Christopher's, but he had seen a lot and done a lot in his short life. A heavy-set African American male, he was born and raised in Brooklyn. Jeremy never knew his father. His mother raised him on her own in a neighborhood rife with drugs, guns, and overall poverty. At age thirteen he stopped going to school. At fourteen he stopped coming home at night, only occasionally popping into the apartment to refuel on food. From the clothing he wore, the kids he hung out with, and his general attitude, his mother knew he was dealing drugs. At fifteen she went to Family Court and took out a Person in Need of Supervision (PINS) petition. Her argument to the judge was that she had lost control of her son. The streets now owned him.

"He is either going to get killed or kill someone. Please get him out of my home and this neighborhood," she begged.

The judge agreed and sent Jeremy to St. Christopher's.

Most kids took at least six months to adjust to our program. Since they are used to doing what they want to do, when they want to do it, they have a hard time following structure and taking directions from adult authority figures. Jeremy was the same way. He tried to use his physical size to intimidate his peers and even the staff. He had a quick mouth and resisted even the basic routines of making his bed, cleaning his room, and doing chores. At one point he tried to get other kids to form a gang right at St. Christopher's.

But we could see another Jeremy underneath the veneer of this one. We continued to bombard him with one consistent message: "You don't have to live the life you've been leading. You are a good person. You have many gifts and skills that you can put to good use for yourself and others."

Eventually the message sunk in. He stopped hassling the staff and other kids, attended school every day, and studied when he got back to his cottage. His grades improved. We put him in charge of our on-grounds store and there he successfully applied the business skills that had once made him an accomplished drug dealer. He joined our varsity track team and threw the shot put.

The average length of time in our program was eighteen months, and when he was nearing that time period Jeremy made it clear that he was not transferring to a group home. He wanted to go home, to be with his mother. We called her in for a series of meetings, some with her and our staff, while others included Jeremy. He was very clear on his end of things: "Mom, I want to go home." She wavered, sometimes telling him, "Just a few more months and you can return," while telling us privately, "I don't think he's really changed. I'll lose him to the streets and the gangs again."

Eventually Jeremy caught on to his mother's shifting point of view. Frustrated to the point of despair, he sent her the following letter, with a carbon copy to me.

Dear Mom,

I'm writing you to express my feelings. I feel very sad, hurt and also a little rejected because it seems to me that you are saying one thing to me and telling the staff here something different. You led me to believe that if I stayed out of trouble, promised to go to school, and behaved myself, I could come back home. In August when we had the meeting I was on Level 3.0 and now I'm on Level 4.3 and still moving up. [We had a behavior management level system at the program; Level 4 was the top level.] *I haven't gotten into any trouble and I'm really trying to do good! I have been controlling my temper and working hard to make sure our home visits together have been good. I want you to try to meet me half-way. I am willing to continue my good behavior and if I don't keep up my end of the bargain I will go back into the program without any arguments. I am saying this because I know we will be okay. All I want to do is get back the wonderful, loving, thoughtful, and caring mother I now realize I lost. And give you back the son you lost to the streets. I want to be home with you to show you that you did not mess up. I am saying this because I know I will be able to stay home with you. Please talk to the staff and work out an agreement that will allow me to come home. I give you my word, I will not disappoint you.*

Your son,
Jeremy

His letter convinced her. She agreed to take him back home. She took a leap of faith and believed that Jeremy had changed and would not return to his old ways.

That priest I heard years ago was right. If you believe in God, you have to believe that people are not locked into their past behavior. In this case, because we the staff believed Jeremy could change, that he was a better person than his activities on the street demonstrated, he began to believe he could change. And once he believed it, he did change. Today, nine years after he left St. Christopher's, he is a counselor there.

Dealing with Death

For those young people who have already experienced much loss in their lives, the loss of someone else they love and admire only adds to the sadness and torment they already feel. Some react by falling even further into themselves, manifest in depression. For others, the loss only fuels the rage that lies dormant beneath the surface. They alleviate their pain through violence and aggression. It can be frightening to watch, and difficult to heal.

One evening in October 1996 I invited Mona Warren and another of our campus supervisors, Art Reid, out to dinner to discuss how things were going in the program. It was a good meeting. I returned home after it was over, and so did Mona. Art went back to work on campus.

About a half hour later Art called me at home on my work phone.

"Did you hear that there was a murder in town today?" he asked.

"What?"

"Yes," he continued, "somewhere in the north end."

There had been a murder the year before in Dobbs Ferry; someone tried to hold up an insurance office and ended up killing a worker there. The police caught the perpetrator. That had been the first murder in town in twenty years. Dobbs Ferry was a very quiet suburban town. A look at the weekly police blotter in the local paper would reveal an occasional DWI or a minor theft, but that was it. Dobbs Ferry was a place families moved to in order to escape from the crime of New York City. So I was surprised that only one year later another homicide had occurred. I planned to watch for it on the 10:00 P.M. news.

I hung up with Art and phoned my sister on Long Island to say hello. We chatted for a few minutes when my work phone rang again. I asked her to hold on while I took the call. It was Art again.

"The police are here and they want to speak with you."

I told him I'd be right over, and then said to my sister, "It's probably nothing. I'll call you right back." And I meant it; the police were often at our place for routine matters, and as director I was the one who dealt with them.

I walked over to the campus and a police lieutenant was there waiting for me. I knew him well. We had a good working relationship and respected each other.

"What's up, lieutenant?" I asked him.

"I need you to come down to the hospital with me," he answered.

"Why?"

"Did you hear there was a murder in town today?" he continued.

"Yes I did."

"Well, we need you to identify the body. We think it's someone you know."

I couldn't believe what I was hearing.

He then produced a motor vehicle report for a black Camaro, registered to Charles Campbell.

"Do you know who this is?" he asked.

"Yes."

Charles Campbell worked for us part time in our recreation department. Mona Warren was his supervisor.

I was in shock. I couldn't believe what I was hearing. I told the lieutenant I'd go with him, but I needed one minute. I ran in to see Art.

"I think you should sit down," I told him.

He did so.

"Remember when you told me about someone being murdered in town today? Don't tell anyone, but it may be Charles Campbell."

"What?" he screamed.

"I don't know for sure," I said, "I'm going with the police now to the hospital." Art sat there with his head in his hands.

The lieutenant drove me to Dobbs Ferry Community Hospital. As we drove I stared out the window looking at the quiet streets of our town. It was hard for me to believe that someone would take another person's life here in Dobbs Ferry. I became accustomed to violence when I worked in low-income neighborhoods of New York City. But here? And Charles Campbell? He was one of the nicest, gentlest people I had ever met in my life. An African American man in his thirties, he had been employed at our program for almost seven years. He worked full time for the White Plains Sanitation Department and for us part time. He was part of our recreation department, organizing basketball games with the kids, softball, kickball, volleyball, and taking them on trips to the movies, bowling alleys, and the like. He was in great physical shape, obviously a body builder. He was very warm, always smiling, with a pleasant personality. The kids adored him, nicknaming him Chazz. I never heard him yell at a young person. He never put them down. He showed them respect, and they in turn respected him.

We entered the hospital and took the elevator down to the basement level. The lieutenant and other officers led me down the hall and to a room marked "Morgue." My stomach sank.

"Lieutenant, can you go in first and look and tell me how bad it is, what to expect?"

I have a weak stomach for physical violence. I don't even like it in movies; I would not go see *Saving Private Ryan* in a theater because I didn't want to view the opening war scene.

He agreed to my request, went into the room for a second, and then came out. He looked grim but said, "You can handle it, Mark. Please go in."

I went in and immediately recognized Charles Campbell. His body lay on a metal table, face up, a white sheet covering him, with only his face exposed. His eyes were wide open. His face was bruised and cut. He had the look of shock on his face. His mouth was open slightly, as if he had died while trying to speak.

"That's Charles Campbell," I said. I walked out and for some reason asked for a second look. I think I was hoping that somehow I was wrong, that that wasn't really Charles lying there. But I wasn't wrong. It was definitely him.

In the hallway I asked the lieutenant, "Why did you have me identify the body? Why not someone from his family?"

"We couldn't locate any of them," he said, "which means you cannot tell anyone back at work. We have to find the family and let them know first."

The police drove me back to campus. Even though I was pledged to secrecy, I went into Art Reid's office and told him the bad news. He was distraught. "I can't believe this," he kept repeating. When I went home I called Mona Warren, but she wasn't home. I asked her son to make sure she called me no matter what the time. Several hours later she returned my call and burst into tears when I gave her the bad news. I asked her to come in first thing in the morning to help me break the news to staff and kids.

That night, word was spreading around campus that it might have been Charles who was killed. Staff started calling me at home. "Was it him? We heard you know." I just told them I couldn't really say.

The New York television networks all ran the story on the 11:00 P.M. news, complete with shots of the black Camaro. They never mentioned Charles by name, but any of our staff watching the news would quickly recognize his car and realize it was he who had been killed. The networks also started to report how the murder occurred. He was shot in a dispute over a parking space.

Earlier that day Charles came to our program to pick up his paycheck. I remember seeing him drive off at around 4:00 P.M. Apparently he drove to the bank to cash it, and ran into one of our social workers who chatted with him. He then drove down the road for a slice of pizza. At this particular pizzeria there are no parking spaces, so Charles did what a lot of people do. He parked in the lot across the street, which was reserved for patrons of a deli and liquor store. He then walked over to the pizzeria. He bought a slice and was walking back to his car when the owner of the deli saw him and came at him screaming and yelling. He was angry that Charles had parked there without buying anything from his deli. The owner was a man in his sixties, who I later learned had a reputation for blowing up on people who parked in his lot without going inside his deli. It turned out the police had recorded numerous complaints against him for harassment.

The owner, according to witnesses, got up into Charles's face. Charles argued back, and at that point two other men came out of the deli and joined the owner. One was a young man, large in stature, the owner's son, a New York City policeman who happened to be in his father's deli at that moment. The other man was the owner's son-in-law. The argument quickly became physical as the three men attacked Charles and threw him to the ground. They pummeled him with their fists and kicked him. Charles managed to get up, run to his car, and grab his cell phone. They wrestled the cell phone from him and smashed it over his head. Charles made it back to his car again and grabbed one of the softball bats he carried from his recreation job at our place. The deli owner and son-in-law tried to wrestle it from him, while the son ran back into the deli. He grabbed his father's .32-caliber Colt automatic and shot Charles three times in the upper body. The son then went back into the deli and told a customer who had witnessed the incident, "Shut up, you didn't see a thing."

Someone called the police, who showed up almost instantly. They arrested the three men, and an ambulance took Charles to the hospital where he was pronounced dead on arrival.

Senseless. Idiotic. Evil.

When I turned on the news the next morning the networks were identifying Charles as the murder victim. The police had apparently contacted his family, which I later learned consisted of his brother, his fiancée, and a twelve-year-old son. I walked over to the campus administrator on duty and asked him if the kids knew that Charles had been killed. He told me they did not. I asked him about one girl with whom Charles was very close, a thirteen-year-old named Vanessa.

"No, she doesn't know," he told me.

Mona showed up, and I asked her to help me break the news to Vanessa. She was Hispanic, unattractive, and overweight. The kids teased her a lot. Her self-esteem was extremely low. She frequently acted out, cursing at staff she didn't like, and annoying the other kids, which then resulted in their teasing her even more. It was like a vicious cycle she didn't know how to get out of. To make things even worse, her mother had died of AIDS while Vanessa was living with us. Vanessa had led a sad life.

Charles was the one person who had been able to connect with Vanessa. He made her feel special probably just by speaking to her with respect. She behaved better when he was around. She dropped her defenses. She didn't feel a need to play the role of the tough, nasty kid with him. We knew she'd be devastated by the news of his death. It would be another loss for a child who had already lost so much.

We asked Vanessa's staff to escort her over to my office. When she arrived, Mona and I sat down with her. We asked her if she had heard about someone dying in Dobbs Ferry the day before. She said yes, and we asked if she knew who it was. When she said no, Mona said, "Vanessa, I have something terrible to tell you. It was Mr. Campbell." There was only silence in the room for a moment. I looked at Vanessa, and there was just this blank look on her face—no anger, no crying, no rage, nothing. Mona put her arm around her and told her that Chazz was with God and that he was praying for her and always would. The three of us stayed there for a few minutes—no words, just quiet. Then Mona asked Vanessa if she was going to be all right. She nodded yes.

Vanessa's staff took her back to her cottage, while Mona started going around to the other cottages to tell staff and kids the terrible news. I hooked up with Luis Medina, our executive director, and other St. Christopher's administrators, to start handling the media, which quickly began descending on our facility. Newspaper reporters, TV anchors—they started appearing in droves. Everyone wanted to know what kind of person Charles Campbell was. I told them that I knew him to be an extremely kind and compassionate person who cared deeply about the young people in our program. I had neither seen nor heard of him acting in a violent way, and in seven years he had never been involved in any kind of physical incident with children or adults.

The next few hours went by like a blur. Mr. Medina called in two grief counselors to work with the kids and the staff. None of our youth acted out; everyone just seemed in shock. It was as if there was a communal stunned silence.

Late that afternoon we held a service in our chapel. Our chaplain led it. Mr. Medina, Mona, and I spoke. I told the kids that what happened wasn't right, that I knew Charles Campbell to be a gentle man who, as physically strong as he was, wouldn't hurt anyone.

"If we can take anything from this tragedy," I said, "let it be that each of us make a commitment to live each day to the fullest and appreciate life as much as possible. When Mr. Campbell left here yesterday afternoon to go cash his check, he had no idea his life would be over in a few minutes. And you know what? None of us know how much time we have left. Each day is a gift. Each moment in each day is a gift. By trying to live that way, we honor Mr. Campbell."

Charles's death was still the headline story in the New York media the next day. The shooting was being portrayed as a racial incident since the three men who attacked him were white and he was African American. Incredibly enough, the deli remained open as if nothing had happened. All three men were out on bail, and the father who had started the entire chain of events was actually back behind the deli counter serving customers.

The kids continued to handle the tragedy admirably. So did the staff, although their stunned silence quickly gave way to anger. Many of the staff at St. Christopher's were African American. They were furious over what had happened to Charles.

"How many black men are going to have to die before this country wakes up?" asked one of our workers. "We had Rodney King a few years ago, then the kid killed by a cop in Washington Heights because he threw a football at his car.

When is this going to end?" His sentiments echoed those of many others at our program.

A "Charles Campbell Committee for Justice" was formed by civil rights activists in the county. I joined it, along with many members of our staff. The Committee decided to hold a march through town that Saturday, ending at the site of the murder. I decided to join and brought my nine-year-old son with me. There were about one hundred people marching, including staff from our program and even some of our kids. Norm Siegel, president of the New York Civil Liberties Union showed up, a few politicians were there, and many civil rights activists. All the networks were filming the event as were the major papers. The Dobbs Ferry police escorted us on the march, which was peaceful. One of our staff led the rally cries and asked different people to speak. They talked about Charles and the kind of person he was. They spoke about the injustice of the incident and their determination to pursue justice through our legal system. Charles's older brother got up and thanked people for their expressions of sympathy and compassion. All this took place while customers went in and out of the deli. But every time someone did, the crowd would plead, "Don't go in. There are murderers in there!"

After several speeches, I was chatting with someone when I thought I heard my name mentioned. I turned to Art Reid and asked him if I he had heard my name.

"Yes," he replied, "It was just announced that you will say a few words."

I didn't have anything prepared, so I stood on top of a parking bumper and delivered an impromptu speech. I thanked everyone for showing up and then said, "It wasn't right what happened. When I went to the hospital that night and found out that Charles Campbell had been killed, I couldn't believe it.

He was such a gentle, nonviolent person. He wouldn't hurt anyone. Justice has to be done. Let justice roll like a mighty river."

The rally ended, but the movement for justice did not. The Committee decided that a rally would be held every Saturday in front of the deli until a trial was held and a guilty verdict returned. Al Sharpton showed up for several of them. So did I. I felt it was important to maintain a witness to what had happened there. Meanwhile, the criminal justice system moved ahead, however slowly. The deli owner and his son-in-law were charged with assault, the son with murder. I knew it would take a year for the case to come to trial, and that it would be a major media event when it did. Staff at our program predicted that if the son was found not guilty there would be a racial explosion in the county. I had my doubts that he would be convicted, and even one of the politicians in the county told me in a private conversation that he felt the same way. The son was, after all, a New York City policeman, and there was a history of difficulty in convicting a policeman of murder in New York.

Eventually the case came to trial. The son's defense was that he was protecting his father, that when he saw Charles with the bat he believed his father's life was in danger. But the prosecutor put on the stand a number of witnesses, including the people who owned the pizzeria across the street, all of whom testified that the three men had savagely beaten Charles. They testified that in their opinion Charles took the bat from his car only as a way to defend himself, and had been backing away and begging for his life when the son shot him.

The son was convicted. His sentence was twenty years to life. The father and brother-in-law were found not guilty. How ironic that the father who, because of his temper, started the whole tragic mess, got off scot-free. I don't know how he lives with himself, knowing that because of his foolishness, because of a parking space, one man is dead and his own son is in jail. I could not bear the guilt of that.

The father runs that deli to this day. Some people have no remorse.

I don't believe it was God's will that Charles Campbell be struck down so cruelly in the prime of his life, leaving so many loved ones behind. But I do believe that God always brings good out of all tragedies. In many ways Charles's death brought the staff together in a way we had not been before. His death united us. We worked together as more of a team, not only in our pursuit of justice for Charles, but in our work at St. Christopher's with the kids. It was strange, but prior to this incident I had tried all kinds of team-building exercises and read many different books on team building and how to get workers to cooperate with and rely on each other more. None of these things came close to uniting us the way Charles's death did. And when I think about it, it reflects the Paschal mystery— how the death of one man on a cross, also innocent, also cut down in the prime of his life, united all of us, all of humanity.

Hope

By my fourth year at St. Christopher's, the program had improved vastly. In fact, it was almost unrecognizable, physically and in every other way. What made the difference? It was due in part to the skilled counselors and therapists we brought in who were able to help our teenagers talk about their lives and thus heal their deep wounds. Renovating the cottages, creating decent and comfortable places for them to live, made a big difference. Promoting Mona Warren to be our Recreation Director, and offering positive, pro-social activities for kids to engage in, meant a lot. Recruiting a chaplain, who ran interdenominational Sunday services in our chapel and formed a gospel choir comprised of our young men and women, made a big difference. Hiring a Domestic Violence coordinator who ran twelve-step groups for our kids on this important issue; starting substance abuse groups; forming volleyball, basketball, and track teams that competed against county high schools; recruiting mentors for our kids; obtaining a federal Housing and Urban Development grant to teach our young people construction trades; securing a county grant that provided summer employment for all our kids; all these factors worked in unison to make St. Christopher's a wonderful place for turning around the lives of troubled adolescents.

But it was more than that. It was teaching our staff to treat young people with dignity and respect, to show them love and affection, and to build relationships with them. It was helping the staff to see that the kids were not the enemy, helping them to understand that in so many ways the kids were victims of their own tormented and confused upbringing. It was helping staff to see that when teenagers acted out and went off, nine times out of ten it was due to fear and self-loathing. Our job was to penetrate beyond that, using the power of love and relationship, to help heal the heart of that child. But most importantly of all, we never gave up hope on any of these kids. This, more than anything else, brought about tremendous change in the lives of these young people.

The following teenagers were all residents of St. Christopher's at some point during my five years there. All of them came to us as "impossible cases." We refused to see them as such. We were able to help turn their lives around.

Randy arrived on our campus at age fourteen. He had been expelled from five New York City public schools during the previous two years. He had been suspended countless times for threatening peers and teachers, and one time for brandishing a razor. We found out he had spent the first three years of his life living in a house with his mother and grandparents; his father was nowhere to be found. His mother was forced from the home for abusing drugs. His grandmother died a few years later, so his grandfather tried to raise both Randy and his brother. When his grandfather passed away, the two boys went to live with an aunt. Randy's brother did well with the aunt, but Randy had trouble getting along with her. According to a psychiatric evaluation, he "refused to listen, was verbally abusive and destructive...admits he wouldn't do chores and was breaking things around the house." The aunt filed a PINS petition with Family Court, and Randy entered the New York City child welfare system.

Randy was initially placed in a diagnostic center, which is a short-term holding facility where a child is evaluated as to what type of placement is needed (i.e., foster boarding home, group home, residential treatment center, or psychiatric hospital). Randy did not do well in the diagnostic center. He assaulted staff, fought with other kids, pulled a kitchen knife on another resident during a dispute in a basketball game, and twice took off his belt in an effort to hit a counselor with it. A psychiatrist at the center described Randy as "needy, angry and depressed...has not developed bonds with anyone so it's difficult for him to trust people. He has experienced himself as unloved and mistreated. His mother was unavailable to him. He perceives the world as depriving and hostile." When given Rorschach ink blots to look at, Randy described "somebody trying to kill somebody," "a mess from a shoot-out," and "a man killing a girl." The diagnostic center psychologist described Randy as "tense, impulsive, immature...wants things his way...extraordinarily strong aggressive impulses...a very difficult, defiant youngster."

And so he was when he arrived on our campus. He was not easy to deal with at all. He constantly tested the staff and tried to deviate from the norms of the campus whenever he could. I remember one specific incident when he was high one night and led a group of boys on a rampage, breaking right through a girl's window and into her room. The girl and her roommates fled while Randy and his peers laughed.

But we hung in there with Randy. Whenever he acted out like that, there were consequences for him—a missed recreation trip, decrease in allowance, no day pass that weekend, and so on. Randy needed structure, desperately, and we were able to provide it for him. He also needed therapy, and we provided that for him weekly. I never asked for any details from Randy or his therapist, but I presume they worked on issues of loss and abandonment and the anger Randy felt from this. In time, the staff in his cottage could really see him change. There were no more wild acts, fewer outbursts, and he began to show respect for peers and for adults. At his annual psychiatric evaluation he said he was proud that he was now in tenth grade and that his goal was to go on to college and then to law school so he could help people. Randy was later elected by his peers on campus to the Leadership Council, which was the youth governing body for the program. He became the star center of the varsity basketball team. He eventually applied to and was accepted in the Job Corps. The psychologist who conducted his final evaluation stated that Randy "appears to get along well with most people...speaks proudly of his non-use of drugs and alcohol, even though most of the peers from his neighborhood do use these."

Janet entered the child welfare system when her mother took out a PINS petition due to her constant staying out late and refusal to follow any of her mother's rules. When Janet ran away for a twenty-five-day period, that was the straw that broke the camel's back for her mom, who was a single parent and a recovering alcoholic. Janet's dad passed away when she was twelve; he was a highway maintenance repair worker who was hit and killed by a sanitation truck.

Janet was sent to a diagnostic center at the age of thirteen and was described by a psychologist there as "very depressed...uncooperative and hostile...has extremely poor impulse control...." She was sent from there to a residential treatment center where a psychiatrist described her as "inappropriate and disruptive...craves excitement and disruption...most enthusiastic in exhorting girls in their complaints and bitterness...this seems to be her highest priority." Staff reported her to be someone who "lies, steals, rarely attends school on grounds, is restless, has masochistic outbursts and frequently goes AWOL." Six months later she had not improved at all, staff at that time describing her as "someone easily led astray by older, negative peers."

Three months later Janet was told that her mother was dying of stomach cancer. Her mother passed away shortly afterward. Her behavior deteriorated dramatically, capped by her theft of an agency car. She led local police in a high-speed, cross-county chase. When caught, she said that it would have been okay if she had killed herself since she had lost her mother and other important people.

Janet was transferred to our campus, now age fifteen. One of our psychologists interviewed her and reported her as "negativistic, brazen, and precocious, with limited understanding of appropriate personal boundaries...a poorly differentiated self-concept...emotionally fragile with a sense of mental confusion...she feels fragmented and incomplete...has a limited ability to relate to others in a healthy manner...has feelings of fear and vulnerability...themes of helplessness, unthinking, impulsive." Cottage staff reported her as easily influenced by negative peers and refusing to do chores.

Like Randy, Janet was not an easy adolescent to deal with, but we stayed the course and arranged for her to see a therapist. It was in therapy that she eventually revealed that her brother had once beaten her and burned her leg with a frying pan. An aunt who was supposed to be taking care of them was too drunk to protect her. The therapist noted that Janet was "plagued by depressed feelings and is suffering quite a lot. It is urgent that she continue in therapy and in the St. Christopher's program to help her deal with the multiple traumas she has experienced."

After eighteen months in our program, Janet was a changed person. She was elected to the Leadership Council. She was always on the highest levels of the Behavior Management

System. Not only did she refuse to follow negative peers, she became a positive leader and role model for new girls on the campus. She made the varsity volleyball squad and won the Most Improved Player award at the end of the season. She was a member of the gospel choir. She eventually left us to move on to a group home, where she attended a neighborhood high school and continued with her goals.

Lily, the fourteen-year-old who helped start the Hayden riot and ended up throwing clumps of grass at me as she lay on the ground faking a knee injury, turned out to be one of our greatest successes. It turned out that Lily had been in and out of the child welfare system since age one. Her mom was a drug addict and died when Lily was eight. Her dad was incarcerated for drug possession when she was ten. She had spent her entire life shifting from foster homes to relatives and back again. She had been expelled from many schools.

Her initial psychiatric evaluation with us described Lily as "chronically depressed with a low energy level, poor coping skills and a negative self-image. She said that she once hurt someone so badly that the person was hospitalized for a week. If granted three wishes, they would be (1) her mom alive, (2) her dad out of jail, (3) more wishes." The official diagnosis was "conduct disorder with underlying depressive disorder, severe psychosocial stressors, and severe impairment with caretakers, peers, school functioning, judgment, thinking and mood."

Lily calmed down somewhat during the next few months, but she was still prone to periodic violent acting-out. Six months after the Hayden riot she was arrested for assaulting one of her peers on campus and placed on probation.

But we continued to work with her, and one year later one of our psychiatrists described her as "open, friendly, has a spontaneous smile. She has good insight and judgment and has learned to control her anger and fighting. She indicates that St. Christopher's has been a good placement because staff has showed her how to handle things differently, and she can talk about her feelings with them. If someone says something derogatory, she doesn't pay any attention. She doesn't get upset as she did in the past. She gets 80s and 90s in school and would like to be a nurse some day. Her three wishes now are (1) get out of placement, (2) move near a former counselor who got married and moved, (3) go to college and become successful."

Lily did phenomenally well in our program. She was always on the highest levels of the Behavior Management System. She was elected to the Leadership Council. Her placement for "Take Our Daughters to Work Day" was at the Westchester County Executive's office and she spent the whole day with the County Executive. A year later he asked that she return.

Lily fully understood our campus philosophy that negative behavior must always be confronted. I can still picture her taking aside a new female resident who was mad at someone and wanted to fight that person. Lily calmly explained to her that this was just not the way things were handled at St. Christopher's. However, the best instance of her confronting negative behavior was when she spotted someone breaking into my house when I was on vacation, told the police, and even identified the man in a lineup. When he was convicted largely on the basis of her identification, the police chief called to tell me they wanted to give Lily a special citizenship award at their annual police dinner. I asked the chief if he remembered arresting her a year earlier for assaulting another youth. He could not believe this was the same girl.

Lily transferred to one of our Westchester group homes, where she continued to do well in school and even became a cheerleader. She is a delightful young woman whom any parent would be proud to have as a daughter.

Henri, fourteen years old when he came to us, was born and raised in Haiti. At age thirteen he was sent to the United States to live with his mother, who resided in Brooklyn and worked as a nurse in a nursing home. He did not handle the transition well. When he wasn't fighting in school, he was truanting and selling drugs. His mother went to Family Court and took out a PINS petition, listing him as uncooperative, disrespectful, and hanging out with a negative peer group.

The psychologist who evaluated Henri when he arrived on our campus described him as having "a very poor self-image ...sees himself as stupid, physically inadequate and infantile. His penchant for immersing himself in the street subculture is likely to be a manifestation of his need to defend against and compensate for these negative feelings about himself. He is highly angry and anxious, quite stimulated by violence. He has a general sense of confusion and disorientation. Limited impulse controls." Henri later told one of our psychiatrists that "he cannot control his anger and may hurt or kill someone. He misses his delinquent friends who sold drugs. In the past he wishes he were never born and has had passive suicidal thoughts."

We found out that Henri was hanging out in his neighborhood with about twenty other teenagers who used drugs and alcohol nightly, and sold crack, marijuana, and cocaine. Henri claims he made about $200 a night and carried a .45 automatic. He frequently took the gun and a knife to school with him, until he just stopped going to school altogether.

Henri ran away from home twice, once for a month. His mother came home one day to find thirty teenagers in the house. She called the police and Henri said he was banished from the house for a month. Henri also claimed he wished to kill his mother's boyfriend, who he said was abusive to her.

Despite Henri's negative history, when asked three wishes he replied (1) get a job in the St. Christopher's maintenance department, (2) graduate from high school and enter the Army, (3) get his own apartment.

After nine months at our program, a psychiatrist reported that "his behavior has improved greatly. He was smoking a lot of marijuana but got a job in the maintenance department and his money is held by staff to go shopping with him. He is not smoking and looks better. His adjustment is good and he is doing pretty well in school. He is polite, friendly and responsive. His mood is friendly. He says everything here is going great and that he has been helped by being at St. Christopher's. He says he has many friends here and he really brightened when he said that he has had a girlfriend for a month and a half."

Ten months later a psychologist wrote that "Henri responds to encouragement. He wants very much to please." Cottage staff, who had initially urged that he be transferred to a more restrictive setting due to frequent stealing, lying, fighting, and drug use, now reported that he was functioning within the program and had learned how to manage his own aggressive behavior. Henri was always one of my favorites, even though my initial encounter was when I had to physically restrain him during a fight with another resident. I spent two days with him at a Ropes Course, and I have a picture on my office wall of Henri helping me scale a wall there.

Henri left us after two years, accepted into the Job Corps, where he did well.

Sonya arrived on our campus, thirteen years old, because of a PINS petition taken out by her mother. The latter had six children ranging from age twenty-six to four months, by several different men. Sonya had no contact with her father; she thought he might be somewhere in Canada. Sonya had scars all over her face, neck, and body. Her mother had scratched her. Sonya told us, "I deserved it."

Sonya had behavior problems in school going back to seventh grade when she started truanting because she felt the rules were too strict. By age twelve she was running away from home for as long as a week at a time. Placed in a residential treatment center, she was kicked out within a month and ended up in a diagnostic center. They described her as "uncooperative, oppositional, indifferent to peers and spends time only with negative ones." The psychiatrist there described her as "sad, with an 'I-don't-care' attitude…anxious, angry, confused and needy…poor self-image and uses poor judgment, can be defiant when not instantly gratified, is mistrustful and testing of authority. She creates distance with peers even though she does want to be liked." The staff at the diagnostic center talked to Sonya's mother by phone and they felt she sounded "overwhelmed and angry."

Sonya started off at St. Christopher's with a bang. Her first week included threatening staff and fighting with a cottage-mate. In the words of our psychiatrist, "she is out of control." He prescribed medication and placed her in our infirmary, where she continued to be "belligerent and difficult." During the next three weeks she tried to assault a peer with a stick, locked herself in our chapel, struck matches to start a fire, vandalized our property, and ended up in a psychiatric hospital for two weeks. Our psychiatrist noted that she "denies, minimizes or rationalizes these things….She has limited insight and judgment of her difficulties."

Upon her return from the hospital, she told us something that the New York City Administration for Children's Services had neglected to let us know when referring her to us: She had been psychiatrically hospitalized twice before, for torching her room and for "catching a tantrum." She then tried to jump out of a cottage window, but was stopped by staff.

We made little progress with Sonya during her first year. Outrageous acts no longer occurred, but she was basically defiant, oppositional with staff, and had very poor socialization skills. Our counselors frequently asked me when we were going to transfer her elsewhere.

Sonya was going to group therapy every week during that first year, and then individual therapy was tried. Within two months the psychologist noted that Sonya was starting to open up, that she was talking about her feelings toward her mother and toward campus staff. "Sonya seems more in control and more cooperative." A month later: "She is calm and pleasant." One month later, Sonya herself was expressing how much more self-control she now had. Cottage staff noted that "she is doing very well in school and performs well in group therapy sessions....She has made a big improvement in the program....She cooperates with staff."

After eighteen months at St. Christopher's, Sonya was a completely different person who was able to control herself and take responsibility for her actions.

Juanito arrived on our campus at the age of thirteen, already having spent time at a number of foster care agencies during his life. His mother was only sixteen when she had him, and Juanito's father was a drug addict who frequently abused the mother. Juanito had school problems early on in life and was hyperactive. He was placed in a residential treatment center at age eight, and stayed eight months. Three years later he was placed on another campus, and then later on in yet a different one. When transferred back home, he would refuse to follow his mother's curfew, and she knew he was hanging out on the streets. By this time his father was in jail for dealing drugs.

Juanito was in a diagnostic center before coming to us. He kept running away from the center, was defiant toward the staff, and bullied younger children. He exhibited much of the same when transferred to us. He was calm much of the time, but when his temper got going, it really got going. I clearly remember Art Reid, our director of youth work, shaking his head after watching Juanito lose it one afternoon. "This kid is really bad news," Art told me.

Juanito ran away from us after only a few months, then suddenly returned seven months later. A few months after that, one of our psychologists described him as "having evidence of depression and internal pain. He hides his emotions and keeps them inside, a defense mechanism to shield himself from pain. He views himself as the cause of his family's problems." The psychologist did see some hope, however. Juanito stated that his goal was to finish high school, go on to college and earn a degree in psychology. "Juanito displays a sense of hope...seems to indicate that he can correct and change his current situation and become a more accomplished, better person." Our psychiatrist agreed. "He is a handsome, cooperative young man who displays a fair amount of poise and apparent emotional openness....He emphasized the gains he has made in his behavior and emotional self-control at St. Christopher's, his acceptance of a greater degree of life responsibility and confidence that he would continue to do well after leaving. He has indeed made some behavioral improvements which reflect an experience of emotional support and structure in the campus program."

Juanito was eventually elected to the Leadership Council and joined our basketball team, where he played as a guard. He held a job in our recreation department. The social worker in his cottage did a lot of work to reconcile Juanito with his mother. He also became close again with his father when the latter was released from prison.

Juanito stayed a little less than eighteen months with us, not getting into one fight during his last twelve months. He told staff that he could now control his temper, that he now knew how to walk away from someone if they made him angry and to instead talk about his feelings with staff or friends. He said he wanted others to see him as someone who is friendly and fun to be with. He also said that he stopped smoking pot while at St. Christopher's.

There was some speculation that Juanito would move back with his family upon leaving our program. He decided against it, however. He said that all his neighborhood friends were now either dead or in jail for dealing drugs, and that he'd feel a lot safer in our group home in Tarrytown. That is where he went. Before leaving, he told our psychiatrist that St. Christopher's "...helped me become a real person. It was a positive experience that will allow me to achieve more in the future." When asked what his three wishes were, he responded: (1) live with his mother at some point in the future, (2) be rich, (3) get rid of guns and drugs so the world could be a better place.

When Tamara arrived at our program, we learned that her mother was very ill with AIDS. Tamara was only twelve and looked even younger. She had been living with her mother and stepfather but kept staying out late, stealing from family and friends, and had all kinds of problems in school. Her mother could not handle her and sent Tamara to live with an aunt. The aunt had no better luck, so into the child welfare system she went.

At a diagnostic center, Tamara required continuous staff supervision, and she was antagonistic and aggressive toward peers. She stole from residents and staff, constantly lied, often had to be physically restrained and, according to center staff, "had no control over her inappropriate behavior."

The diagnostic center was able to fill us in on Tamara's tumultuous family history. Her mother had been a drug addict and prostitute. She took Tamara and her other two daughters to North Carolina when Tamara was only two. They stayed there for five years, but Child Protective Services removed the children due to abandonment. The daughters lived with various relatives. All reported Tamara as being uncontrollable, often fighting peers, refusing to follow curfew, and having verbal and physical outbursts. A psychiatrist at the diagnostic center evaluated her right before she came to us. "She is depressed, insecure, anxious, and has experienced much emotional deprivation and rejection."

Tamara introduced herself to our program by holding a lit match to another girl's foot while the latter was asleep. She did this to several different girls in the cottage during her first two weeks. She finally stopped, although for the next few months she continued to threaten to do it. She did do things like assault staff and peers, threaten to kill staff, severely scratch a girl's face in school, bite a staff member on the leg, expose her breasts in school, and rub Vaseline on her private parts openly in the cottage. She also had the habit of stealing something from one girl, placing the item in another girl's room, and then watching them fight about it.

Eight months later she was still doing things like putting a cigarette lighter to an aerosol can to create a torch. Staff reported her as being oppositional, refusing to get out of bed in the morning, and refusing to wash. A few months later she and two other new female residents went AWOL from our campus and ended up in a crack house in the city. We sent two of our most street-smart male staff to go and get them. The men were successful but came back frightened and vowing never to go back. I was called over to Tamara's cottage the next night because she was packing her things to go back to the crack house. I personally wrestled her to the ground and restrained her until she calmed down. We convinced her that we weren't going to let her return there.

Tamara's mother continued to deteriorate during this entire time, and we believed that was the reason for all the acting-out.

We sent Tamara and two other residents whose mothers were dying of AIDS to a special group in Westchester that met weekly. This appeared to have a calming effect on her. We also placed her in Hayden Cottage, which by now had been transformed by Linda Rodgers into our best cottage. Tamara did well under the structured environment there, to the point where one of our psychiatrists even noted that her "overall behavior is improving....She is involved in few negative incidents."

Her mother passed away in Tamara's eighteenth month at our program. Tamara handled it well. I went to the wake and was convinced that the group counseling to which we had sent her had paid off. In the months that followed, Tamara continued to calm down and behave much better. She joined the choir. She became a young lady.

It is essential to maintain hope, no matter how far gone a young person may seem. Without hope, we fall into despair. And when we despair, we give up, we stop trying to make a difference.

Fight despair. Do not give up on any child. Ask God for the strength to hope, for the strength to stand by a young person who is struggling.

Remembering What Is Important

It is very easy for adults to forget what is important in life.

It's easy for parents to forget that being faithful and loving to your spouse; knowing and loving your children in as rich a way as possible; growing in your relationship with God; helping the poor and marginalized; and working to create a more peaceful and just world are really the only things that matter.

It's just as easy for teachers, youth ministers, mentors, and pastors to forget the same things. We too often get wrapped up in our plans, our ideas, our ambitions, and our opinions. We then fail to see that which is of the greatest urgency—the present moment, the people right in front of us, and their needs.

Every spiritual tradition teaches that only in the present moment can pure joy be found. The Christian tradition is no different. Jesus told his followers, "The Kingdom of God is here, now, present among you." He tried to shake people out of their ideologies and their fixed ways of thinking, out of their agendas, out of their resentments over the past and worries about the future. He tried to get them to come alive to the glory of the present moment and all it contains.

I have found that young people can do this for us. They wake us up, alerting us to what is really important in life.

"Are the computers fixed yet, mister? Can we get onto the Internet now?"

Fernando, again. He is twelve-years-old and one of thirty-four young people mandated by Juvenile Court to attend our juvenile justice center. Fernando and his peers come to the center for counseling, tutoring, mentoring, anger management classes, and to participate in adult-supervised activities and recreation. This is my third time at the center within the last ten days, trying to fix the computers there. And each time Fernando greets me with the same question: "Are they fixed yet?"

I'm not even a computer specialist. Far from it. After leaving St. Christopher's in 1998 I became the associate executive director of the Domus Foundation, a nonprofit organization in Stamford, Connecticut, that oversees this center and five other programs for at-risk youth. I was in charge of the Domus finance department and quality improvement. I obtained state and city grants and wrote proposals so Domus can open up new programs for at-risk youth. I served on a state-wide committee representing the concerns and interests of low-income children and families. Fixing two malfunctioning computers was never in my job description when I joined Domus, but without the funds to hire a computer specialist, I am left to do it. I know that if I don't repair them, no one else will, and kids will not have access to the Internet, which we believe is necessary for them to do well in school.

So here I am again: downloading an antivirus program, which keeps calling for a reboot disk that no one at the center can find; trying to get past a password that a former counselor at the center installed a long time ago; calling our Internet provider to try and find out if the problem is at their end and not ours. A bead of sweat rolls down my brow, for it is hot in the center today, and resentment starts to grow. "I can't believe I'm stuck doing this," I whisper to myself, followed by the thoughts, "I have a master's degree....I should be an executive director by now....I should be working at a place where I could delegate this to somebody." I think of people I graduated with from college, and the positions they now hold in law, medicine, and business. One of them is the governor of the very state I am working in.

Fernando returns.

"Fixed yet?"

"No," I tell him, as I keep my simmering anger in check. No need to take it out on him. Unlike most of the kids in the program, he was never arrested, he is not on probation or parole. His mother died a year ago, and he has been having a hard time ever since. He never knew his biological father, and now lives alone with his stepfather. He is overweight and looks even younger than his age. I can see he does not interact with the other kids very well; I imagine that when staff members are out of sight he is easily scapegoated by his peers. I ask his case worker if he is developmentally disabled in any way, and she says no, but he is unable to read. She shows me his case file, in which it is reported that since his mother died Fernando sometimes hears voices. His stepfather referred him to our program because Fernando was staying out late at night, he doesn't know with whom, and he is worried Fernando will start using drugs and get into trouble. On top of it all, Fernando moved to this country only a year ago. His stepfather is an immigrant from the Dominican Republic, very poor, and does not have the money for the therapy Fernando needs to help him cope with the loss of his mother. His father has turned to us. We will do our best to help Fernando.

Fernando leaves the room when I tell him the computers are still not operating, but a few minutes later I click the Outlook Express icon, hear a dial tone, hold my breath as "Verifying

Username and Password" pops up on the screen, and, yes, finally, there it is, the homepage for Microsoft Network. I turn to the other computer, duplicate the ritual, and it too connects. I can hardly believe it.

I poke my head out of the computer room and call for Fernando.

"Yo, Fernando, take a look at this."

He rushes over and when he sees the two screens, he is overjoyed, I mean literally overjoyed.

"Thank you, mister, thank you!" he keeps repeating, shaking my hand continuously. He seats himself at one of the terminals and starts clicking away. I begin packing up, on to my next project within another part of Domus.

Then something funny happens, a small thing but something I will probably never forget. Fernando takes a break from the screen, turns to me and says, "You're a kind man."

And with that remark any lingering resentment about my job, my responsibilities, and my status in this or any other organization burns away. And I immediately think about something I read by St. Francis de Sales: "Do not bother yourself about whether or not what God asks of you is important and grand. Whether your actions are insignificant or not does not matter, if they are God's will."

And it suddenly becomes very clear to me that while it is fine to have career goals and to aspire to certain things in life, it is infinitely more important to be attentive to the people and tasks right in front of you. Position and rank within an organization mean very little. Money means very little. But repairing two computers so a boy who recently lost his mother and is struggling in a new country can have a little enjoyment and perhaps even learn to read—that means a lot.

Parents—please take time each day to think about what is important in life. Communicating with your children, telling them how much you love them, going to church with them on Sunday, attending their soccer games—these things are all important. Making a lot of money, making it to the top of your company, and your golf game are not that important. So much in life comes down to choices. Please make the right choices, for the sake of your children and for the sake of your own emotional and spiritual life.

Teachers, counselors, and ministers—you have been given a tremendous responsibility. Don't let ambition or trivialities obscure the reality that Christ lives within all of us, including and especially the children placed in your care. Let every day, every interaction with a young person, reflect the seriousness with which you regard your vocation. Always remember to treat young people with the respect and dignity they deserve. The way you speak to them is the way you speak to God.

Appendix: Points for Discussion

Discussion Questions by Chapter

Commitment

- What do you think led Tony to abandon a seventeen-year career of drugs and crime? What part do you think the author played in Tony's decision to go straight?

- Do you think it was strictly coincidence that the author learned about Tony being in jail after a five-year absence from each other, or was God somehow behind that? Are there "coincidences" that have occurred in your life that you can now look and see God's hand at work?

- Are there people in your life who have disappointed you and who you have written off because of this? Would it be possible to reconnect with some of these people if they need help now?

Role Model

- Why did Marge have such an effect on the author? What qualities did she possess which so impressed him?

- In what ways was Jesus a role model for his disciples? Can you think of specific instances in the Gospel when Jesus served as a role model?

- Who are the role models you look up to in your life? In what ways do they guide you? Are there ways you could be serving as a positive role model for others in your community, school, workplace, and family?

Taking It Seriously

- Do you think the author was right in his decision not to allow this young man to return to Covenant House?

- This story is about the balance between two Christian values—mercy and fairness. Is it possible to show mercy to one particular person while also exhibiting fairness to the group?

- Have there been times in your life when you were torn between trying to help someone in need while being fair to others?

Forgiveness

- In this story, the author chose to keep in contact with Santos even though he had murdered one of his coworkers. Was this the right thing to do? What do you think influenced the author to do so?

- Jesus told his disciples to forgive "seventy-seven times" (Matt 18:22) if necessary. Do you think he meant this literally? Is this kind of forgiveness realistic in a world such as ours?

- Are there people in your life whom you have not yet forgiven because they did something which hurt you? What stops you from reaching out to these people?

Honesty

- Do you think Joe will be able to put an end to his history of conning and trying to fool people? Why do you think this female counselor was able to get through to him?

- Who are the people in the Gospel who try to fool Jesus, who try to trip him up with verbal sparring? How does he react to them?

- Have there been times in your life when you were not fully honest with someone, even conning them? In what ways can you live your life more truthfully, as Jesus did?

Faithfulness

- Hector, Antoine, and Titus each decided to forego the help that was being offered them and to instead return to street life. Why do you think they made this decision?

- How do you think Jesus dealt with discouragement in his ministry, when others misunderstood his message or even misunderstood him?

- How do you deal with discouragement in your life? How do you deal with the temptation to give up on people or on projects that you believe are important?

Perseverance

- Why does the author find solace in Thomas Merton's "Letter to a Young Activist" in response to the two letters he discovers after so many years?

- In the parable of the "Sower and the Seed" Jesus talks about a planter who continues to plant seeds by the road-side and among the weeds, hoping they will somehow take root. Can you see how this parable might influence the author in his work with troubled youth?

- Can you think of people in your life who, like Carlton, did not show much promise when you first knew them, but who developed new traits that led them to a happy and fulfilling life? Does this story help you to believe that every human being is capable of change and growth?

Leadership

- Were you surprised that the gathering of young people in response to the Rodney King verdict did not turn violent? What prevented it from becoming so?

- Jamel was a young man with a troubled and difficult past, yet God clearly used him in this instance to calm the fears and rage of his peers. Can you think of other people in the Bible, in history, and even today, who had personal difficulties yet were used by God to accomplish good works on his behalf?

- Would you have handled this situation differently than the author (i.e., tried to prevent the rally, made the statement he did at the end, etc.)?

Courage

- Do you think the author handled this situation well? Would you have done anything differently?

- Jesus frequently taught his disciples to pray for courage for those times when they were to be "put to the test." Do you think this was one of those times?

- This incident, following the Rodney King one, must have been discouraging for the author. Can you remember times in your life when you were discouraged, yet you persevered? What gave you the strength to carry on? Was prayer part of that? Do you think God can give a person the ability to survive difficult circumstances such as these the author faced?

Setting Limits

- The author and his coworkers reacted firmly and decisively in the aftermath of the riot. Did they make good decisions in the way they handled the young women in that cottage?

- Jesus was able to stay calm and focused even in the midst of chaos and confusion, as in the time he traveled with his disciples in a boat during a storm. Do you think the author was able to do the same during this ordeal?

- What times in your life have you felt panic and confusion, yet you managed to summon the strength to make good decisions and overcome fear?

Taking a Stand

- There was apparently a culture that permitted violence toward students in this school. How and why does something like this develop? How is it possible to change it?

- Reverend Martin Luther King and Bishop Oscar Romero were two people who stood up against injustices and paid with their lives for it. What do you think motivated them and others like them?

- Both Virginia Smith and the author took a risk by doing what was right. Can you remember people in your life who stood up for what was right, even though it put them at risk of harm or ridicule?

Saving One Another

- Were you surprised that the boys in this story, some of whom had criminal backgrounds, acted with such courage, leadership, and compassion?

- The First Letter of St. John says, "We know love by this, that he laid down his life for us—and we ought to lay down our lives for one another" (1 John 3:16). Isn't that what happened in this story? Why are some people able to put themselves in harm's way to help another person, while others do not?

- Do you think you would have been willing to scale down the ravine and join them in their efforts to save Corinne?

Creating Memories

- Were you surprised when the author changed his mind after his late-night exchange with Keenan?

- Do you think this one weekend skiing experience changed the lives of these boys?

- Have you ever had an experience, even though it was brief, that changed your life? If so, why did it do this for you?

Connections

- This story is actually about a very simple experience—biking with friends and then relaxing afterward. But to these young men it meant so much more. Why?

- Near the end of his life, Jesus told his disciples, "I do not call you servants any longer...I have called you friends" (John 15:15)." Why do you think he said this to them? What was he trying to say to them? Why did Jesus put such a value on friendship?

- Reflecting back on your life, can you remember times like this—simple moments of companionship that did not entail large expenditures of money or lavish plans? Why do these mean so much to us?

Loss

- Reading this story, do you now have a better understanding of the anger and self-destructive tendencies that exist within troubled adolescents like Levon?

- In one of his letters, St. Paul wrote, "Judge no one, lest you yourself be judged." What did he mean, and why did he write this?

- Do you sometimes judge a person based on their external behavior and speech, without understanding what may be taking place behind the scenes, in their family life?

Nonviolence

- Do you really think it is possible to teach young people, who grew up in families and neighborhoods rife with violence, to respond nonviolently?

- What do you think of Jesus' teaching to "turn the other cheek...love your enemies"? Did he mean this literally?

- Who are the modern-day teachers of nonviolence you admire?

Learning from Failure

- Why did the St. Christopher's teenagers react the way they did at Playland?

- How do you think God regards our failures and setbacks?

- Have you had moments of failure and disappointment in your life that later helped you to grow and change for the better?

Faith and Change

- Were you surprised that Jeremy's mother changed her mind and took him back?

- Was the priest quoted in the beginning of the story correct, that to believe in Christ is to believe in the capacity of people to change?

- Have there been times when you judged someone as incapable of change? Does this story help you to see that person differently?

Dealing with Death

- Can you understand the reactions of the teenagers at St. Christopher's to Mr. Campbell's murder?

- Did God bring some goodness out of the death of Charles Campbell?

- Can you think of tragedies that occurred in our country from which God somehow brought forth blessings?

Hope

- What combination of factors led to the turnaround in the lives of these young people?

- In the Gospel, it says that, "[Jesus] saw a great crowd; and he had pity on them, because they were like sheep without a shepherd" (Mark 6:34). How do you think Jesus looked upon the young people whose stories are told in this chapter?

- Can you think of people who at one time seemed hopeless but who are now living happy and fulfilling lives? What caused their turnaround?

Remembering What Is Important

- Why was the author so struck by the brief comment made by Fernando?

- How did Christ work through Fernando to bring about greater understanding and wisdom in the author?

- Have there been times in your life when you were caught up in your own success and achievement? What helped you to recognize this and change, turning back to those things that are really important in life?